Flying the
BUCCANEER

Flying the BUCCANEER

Britain's Cold War Warrior

Peter Caygill

Pen & Sword
AVIATION

First published in Great Britain in 2008 by
PEN & SWORD AVIATION
an imprint of
Pen & Sword Books Limited
47 Church Street
Barnsley
S. Yorkshire
S70 2AS

ISBN 978 1 84415 669 6

A CIP catalogue record for this book
is available from the British Library.

Typeset in Times New Roman
Pen & Sword Books Limited

Printed and bound in England
by Biddles Ltd

Pen & Sword Books Ltd incorporates the imprints of
Pen & Sword Aviation, Pen & Sword Maritime,
Pen & Sword Military,Wharncliffe Local History, Pen & Sword Select,
Pen & Sword Military Classics and Leo Cooper
Remember When, Seaforth Publishing and Frontline Publishing.

For a complete list of Pen & Sword titles please contact:
PEN & SWORD BOOKS LIMITED
47 Church Street, Barnsley, South Yorkshire, S70 2AS, England.
E-mail: enquiries@pen-and-sword.co.uk
Website: www.pen-and-sword.co.uk

CONTENTS

ACKNOWLEDGEMENTS

Much of the information contained in this book has come from official RAF sources held at the National Archives at Kew and I would like to thank the staff for their assistance during the course of my research.

A book of this nature would not have been possible without the personal input of people who were involved with the Buccaneer. In particular I would like to thank Don Headley who, after flying the Vampire, Venom and Javelin with the RAF, became a test pilot with Hawker Siddeley (later BAe) at Holme-on-Spalding Moor and eventually accumulated over 1,000 hours on the Buccaneer. He was also responsible for the Phantom and spent seven years at BAe as Chief Test Pilot of its Brough division. Don's knowledge of testing the Buccaneer is second to none and his recollections of flying it to the extremes of its performance envelope make for fascinating reading.

I am also deeply indebted to Group Captain Tom Eeles who has contributed his experiences during tours flying the Buccaneer with the Fleet Air Arm and the RAF. Having flown Canberras in RAF Germany he was given the opportunity of an exchange posting with the FAA during which he flew with 801 Squadron on board HMS *Victorious*. He then went on to be a flying instructor and as a QFI he taught on 736 Squadron, the Royal Navy Buccaneer conversion unit, before rejoining the RAF and completing four tours on Buccaneers, one with 12 Squadron and three with 237 OCU, the last as its commanding officer. By the time that he had to say goodbye to the Buccaneer Tom had nearly 2,200 hours on type in his logbook. Group

Captain Tom Eeles' autobiography is published by Pen and Sword books entitled 'A Passion for Flying'.

I would also like to thank Captain Alan J. Leahy CBE DSC and Group Captain Mike Shaw CBE. Alan Leahy was one of the first Navy pilots to fly the Buccaneer S.1 when he commanded 700Z Flight, the Intensive Flying Trials Unit at Lossiemouth. This unit was tasked with evaluating the Buccaneer to see exactly what it could do so that it could be used to its full potential. Mike Shaw had a brief association with the Buccaneer in the early 1980s when he was Station Commander at RAF Honington, home of 237 OCU. This was a difficult period for the Buccaneer as the aircraft was grounded for a time following a mid-air break up that had been caused by metal fatigue. Mike describes what it was like at this time and how the Buccaneer bounced back to regain its position as an indispensable element of the RAF's offensive power. Although he has many more hours on the Lightning and Phantom, the Buccaneer still managed to give him one of his worst moments in the air, an event that ended happily for both aircraft and crew and is recounted in the book.

Finally I would like to thank Philip Jarrett for delving into his photographic archive once again to provide a range of illustrations of the Buccaneer throughout its long and distinguished history.

INTRODUCTION

In the period immediately after the end of the Second World War the British aircraft industry managed to produce some outstanding designs, despite the obfuscation and confused thinking that often emanated from their political overlords. One such was the Blackburn B.103 which resulted from a far-sighted Admiralty requirement for a transonic strike aircraft capable of sustained flying at low level. Initially referred to as the NA.39, it was later given the name Buccaneer and was to become, arguably, the finest attack aircraft of its day.

Although its qualities were apparent at a very early stage in the flight test programme, it was not appreciated by all. The 1950s saw a period of rapid improvement in terms of performance and the capability of military aircraft, with the World Absolute Speed Record being raised on a regular basis. There was a fascination with speed and supersonics in particular, a mood that was prevalent not only in the general public, but in a number of Air Staffs throughout the world, including the Royal Air Force. This situation was compounded by the emergence of advanced designs such as the swing wing layout, as championed by Sir Barnes Wallis, which could be used to vary the angle of wing sweep in flight. This fixation with supersonics and futuristic-looking designs was to cost the RAF dearly. Had the service not been so obsessed it might have avoided the costly abandonment of the TSR.2 project and the cancellation of the follow-on order for the General Dynamics F-111 variable-sweep, strike/attack aircraft.

While the RAF was heading down the dead end that was

TSR.2, the Navy was getting to grips with the Buccaneer which soon showed that it could fly at just below the speed of sound and carry a greater load over a longer distance than any other aircraft. Although the Buccaneer S.1 with its de Havilland Gyron Junior engines was marginal on power should an engine failure occur at the wrong time, there was no such problem with the S.2 which had Rolls-Royce Speys that offered approximately 50 per cent more power. The Buccaneer was easily capable of yet more development but even after the demise of TSR.2 the Royal Air Force showed no real interest until eventually it became the only alternative. Even so there was a certain amount of resentment at having to fly a Navy machine.

Once in RAF service the Buccaneer soon silenced its critics and it quickly found an enthusiastic following among the crews that had the privilege of flying it. It was in its element at low level where its ability to fly at speeds of up to 580 knots and easily to cope with turbulence became legendary. Even by the time it was retired in 1994, by which time it had been in service for over thirty years, it had still not been bettered and the Buccaneer could easily have continued into the 21st Century had there been a need for it to do so.

This book looks at the Buccaneer from the point of view of the crews that were tasked with flying it. Performance and handling characteristics, together with the results of pre-service trials on land and at sea, are interspersed with first-hand accounts. Also included are the tactics that were devised for the overland penetration and maritime strike missions, plus some of the incidents that befell Buccaneer crews when things did not go according to plan.

Although the Buccaneer was not the most glamorous of aircraft, there can be no doubt that it was ideally suited to its role. It looked formidable, and its excellent handling characteristics and immense strength endeared it to its crews. It is now fifty years since the prototype NA.39 first flew but the memory lives on in the aircraft that have been preserved, particularly those that are kept in 'live' or airworthy condition. At the time of writing only XW986 flies with Mike Beachy Head in South Africa but it is hoped that XX885 will return to the skies in the UK to bring a tear to the eye of those who flew in the Buccaneer and to remind everyone else of its vital role in maintaining the peace during the Cold War.

CHAPTER ONE

Design and Development

The Blackburn Buccaneer came about as a result of a far-sighted naval requirement for a low-level strike aircraft capable of flying at transonic speeds to deliver a tactical nuclear bomb or a range of conventional weapons. What is remarkable is that a need for this type of attack was recognised by the Royal Navy as early as 1952, a time when the major air forces of the world were still thinking in terms of high-flying bombers and were only beginning to consider the threat posed to offensive aircraft by increasingly sophisticated ground-based radars, defensive fighters and the imminent arrival of the first surface-to-air missile systems. In contrast, the Admiralty saw that low level penetration offered the best chance of carrying out a successful mission, as a surprise attack made under an enemy's radar cover significantly increased the attacking aircraft's chances of survival.

This new way of thinking was of great interest to Blackburn Aircraft at Brough on Humberside as the company had a long history of designing and building aircraft for the Royal Navy dating back to the Dart single-engined torpedo-carrier of 1921. Various design studies had already been set in motion for advanced aircraft and one of the prime requirements of these was to cure the phenomenon of 'pitch-up', a problem which particularly affected swept-wing jet fighters of the 1950s. This happened at high angles of attack and was caused by the outer portions of the wings stalling before the inner section due to the spanwise flow of air, an occurrence that, because of the swept wing, had the effect of moving the centre of pressure inwards and forwards and causing the aircraft to 'tuck in' to a turn. This also had a knock-on effect as designers had to be careful in their positioning of the horizontal tail, as any problems with longitudinal stability could result in a 'deep-stall' situation if the tail was mounted on the fin. In this instance the tail could be blanketed by the turbulent wake coming from the wing so that recovery from a nose-high position was impossible. Blackburn's answer to the problem was to design a wing that had a pronounced change in the leading-edge sweep angle, the inboard section of the wing being swept 40 degrees, with the outer portions employing 30 degrees of sweep. With a lessening of thickness/chord ratio on the outer wings and the use of leading slats it was hoped that pitch-up could be avoided.

The Royal Navy requirement for a low-level strike bomber was encapsulated in Specification M.148T. It called for a two-seat aircraft capable of flying at Mach 0.85 at a height of 200 ft and having a radius of action of 400 miles. The principal target was to be the new Soviet Sverdlov-class cruisers which could easily threaten the sea lanes on which Britain depended, however attacks against shore installations were also intended for the new aircraft. Various offensive loads were proposed including two nuclear weapons: Green Cheese, a guided nuclear device, and Red Beard, a free-fall tactical nuclear bomb also referred to as the Target Marker Bomb (TMB). Other armaments quoted in the specification were the carriage of four Red Angel (Special M) bombs, 24 air-to-surface rockets (OR.1099), two 2,000 lb armour piercing (AP) bombs, four 1,000 lb medium capacity (MC) bombs or a 4 x 30 mm Aden gun pack.

As the all-up weight of the aircraft would be around 42-45,000 lb, some means of reducing the approach speed to land on the Navy's carriers was clearly desirable and much thought was given to the principle of jet deflection whereby engine thrust was angled downwards to provide lift. To evaluate this idea a Meteor Mark 4 (RA490) was modified by Westland Aircraft to have two Rolls-Royce Nene jet engines of 5,000 lb thrust. These were mounted forward of the wing leading-edge in extended nacelles so that the deflector nozzles which protruded from the undersides were close to the aircraft's centre of gravity. Although the system incurred a weight penalty, successful trials were carried out at Farnborough and approach speeds were reduced by around 10 knots.

Specification M.148T produced several contrasting designs from Britain's aircraft manufacturers including submissions from Armstrong Whitworth, Fairey, Hawker, Shorts, Westland and Saunders-Roe, in addition to Blackburn. The final three chosen for further evaluation were the Armstrong Whitworth AW.168, Shorts PD.13 and the Blackburn B.103. The AW.168 was rather more conventional than the other two designs and was powered by two de Havilland Gyron Junior engines mounted in nacelles on the wings. Jet deflection was used for take-off and flap blowing, taking high pressure air from the engine compressors, was required for landing at the all-up weight quoted. As the aircraft offered the necessary range and speed, it was a serious contender, especially as it could be offered to the Royal Navy to meet the 1960 deadline for service entry. The Shorts PD.13 was much more advanced than the AW.168 in that it was a tailless design which utilised the 'aero-isoclinic' wing as developed on the SB.1 glider and SB.4 Sherpa. This had rotating tips that together acted as elevators, or in opposition as ailerons. The PD.13 had sharply swept wings and the jet pipes were designed to be lowered to provide jet deflection. Power was provided by two Rolls-Royce Avon RA.19s which offered performance levels in excess of the requirement with a top speed of Mach 1.0.

Although the Shorts PD.13 was technically advanced and the manufacturers were able to commit to its development, there was a high degree of risk with this design, especially with regard to the wing-tip controllers and the jet deflection system. It was also clear that the aircraft could not be produced in time to meet the Navy's requirements and so the PD.13 was discarded. This left just the AW.168 and Blackburn's B.103. The AW.168 was technically the least advanced of all the competitors which meant that its service life was likely to be short as it was incapable of significant development. On the plus side it could be developed quickly, but in recent years Armstrong Siddeley had not produced any of their own designs having instead been engaged in building other manufacturers' aircraft, notably the night-fighter version of the Meteor and the Sea Hawk fighter for the Fleet Air Arm. Despite the fact that the B.103 was also likely to miss the in-service date (in this case by around a year), this was eventually deemed to be acceptable as it offered a reasonable compromise between aircraft capability and development, timescale and design capacity. After deliberating long and hard during the first week of December 1954, the Tender Design Conference came to the conclusion that Blackburn's design was the winner and would be the only aircraft to be produced to Specification M.148T.

The first B.103 design study produced by Blackburn in 1952/53 employed a relatively large wing (650 sq ft) with compound leading edge sweep, a high-mounted T-tail and twin Armstrong Siddeley Sapphire jet engines positioned well forward to allow for jet deflection. By 1954 this design had evolved to have a smaller, mid-mounted wing of around 500 sq ft in area with the engines mounted further back in a more conventional location and blended into the centre section. The use of jet deflection had been abandoned and the principle of 'blown' surfaces was now being proposed to reduce landing speeds. This involved bleeding high-pressure air from the aft section of the engine compressor and blowing it over the lifting surfaces to increase lift and thus allow the aircraft to fly more slowly in the landing configuration. The technique had first found favour in the USA where it was used to blow air over the flaps of aircraft such as the Lockheed F-104 Starfighter to prevent flow breakaway and increase lift. The designers at Blackburn were impressed with the likely benefits but took the idea much further in that engine air was ducted to the entire trailing edge of the wing so that the ailerons (which could also be drooped at low speeds) were blown as well as the flaps. It was not long before the idea was extended so that air was also blown over the leading edge of the wing as well. This not only solved any de-icing problems but also meant that the leading-edge slat could be deleted. Initial testing of a system of boundary

-layer control showed that it was vastly superior to jet deflection and offered nearly double the lift of a conventional 'unblown' wing.

Of course in aviation, as in all other aspects of life, you do not get anything for nothing and the downside was a loss in engine thrust as approximately 10 per cent of the mass flow was tapped to provide the bleed air. This meant that safety was likely to be marginal if an engine was lost when in the landing configuration. In addition, the reaction to downwash from the drooped ailerons and flaps would also cause a significant nose-down pitch. This could have been counteracted by increasing the size of the horizontal tail but this would also have increased weight and drag. To get round these problems Blackburn extended the air bleed system to incorporate an outlet on the underside of the tail from which high-pressure air re-energised the boundary layer to help provide the necessary download to raise the nose. This was done in conjunction with a tab on the trailing edge of the tailplane which moved upwards when the flaps were selected. To counter the extreme heat of the blown air the internal ducting and the outlets had to be made in heat-resisting alloy.

The first outline drawings of the B.103 showed an aircraft with a conventional streamlined fuselage but one which had its greatest cross-sectional area set well forward. By early 1954 this shape had been adapted somewhat as the engine intakes had been moved rearwards and the fuselage was at its deepest at around the mid-point of the wing which was also reduced in area. It was around this time that Richard T. Whitcomb of the National Advisory Committee for Aeronautics (NACA) came up with his area-rule theory in the USA. This stated that to avoid excessive wave drag in the transonic region, a graph showing the cross-sectional area of the fuselage, wings and tail assembly should change in a smooth curve from nose to tail without any sudden variations. The timing of this discovery was perfect as far as the B.103 was concerned, an event that was in marked contrast to the Convair YF-102 delta-winged interceptor in the United States which had to undergo a complete redesign before it could exceed the speed of sound in level flight. Despite the fact that B.103 was designed to cruise at Mach 0.85, any reduction in drag would mean that less power was needed to fulfil its mission and therefore radius of action would not be adversely affected. When Whitcomb's rule had been fully evaluated by Blackburn's design team, their proposed attack bomber emerged with a redefined fuselage with pronounced 'waisting' around the centre section and an enlarged area adjacent to the jet efflux to maintain its cross-sectional curve as a smooth dome shape from nose to tail. This was to be one of the more obvious pieces of area ruling, unlike two other British aircraft of slightly earlier vintage, the English Electric P.1 and Fairey F.D.2 which also complied with the theory but more by accident than design.

Although the initial proposal had indicated the use of a pair of Sapphire jet engines, these were quickly discarded in favour of the de Havilland Gyron Junior as it was hoped that the lower specific fuel consumption of the latter would extend range. The new de Havilland engine was a scaled down version of the Gyron which was first run in 1953 and three years later was producing a massive 25,000 lb thrust in reheat which made it the most powerful jet engine available in the west. The Gyron Junior started bench tests on 12 August 1955 and passed its qualifying test less than a year later. It had been designed from the start to incorporate compressor bleed air for high-lift devices and the thrust that was lost was restored by burning more fuel. This tended to produce higher temperatures in the turbine area with the result that much attention had to be focused on the cooling of the turbine blades. The problems were eventually solved and the engine was cleared for use with a thrust rating of 7,100 lb.

As the aerodynamic design of the B.103 evolved towards its final form, others within the design team at Blackburn were concerned with the main structure which had to be able to withstand the stresses imposed by flight at high subsonic speeds at ultra low-levels and also to provide a suitably long fatigue life. In the areas subject to the highest loads, high-grade steel forgings were used, together with integrally-machined ribs and spars in the wings. The centre of the airframe was made up of three double-ring sections to which the front, rear and auxiliary wing spars were attached, with the jet pipes passing through the openings. Each ring was connected to the adjacent ring on the other side of the aircraft by high-steel frames. A unique, and necessary, feature was the large clamshell airbrake which comprised the extreme rear of the fuselage, aft of the T-tail. Although this was initially designed in response to a dive-bombing requirement, the feature came into its own as it allowed higher power levels to be used during landing which meant that more bleed air was available. Handling was also improved as the minimum drag speed was reduced.

A particularly neat feature was the design of the weapons bay, the door of which was made to rotate through 180 degrees immediately before the store was to be released. As the requirement was to carry a nuclear weapon this had to be accommodated internally and the adoption of a rotating bomb-door avoided unwanted turbulence and drag which would be produced by the use of conventional bomb doors. Wing pylons were also included for the external carriage of drop tanks, bombs and rocket pods. The flying controls were fully powered, the surfaces being operated by two separate hydraulic systems so that if any one system failed there was sufficient power for the aircraft to be flown safely. The controls had to be acceptable over a wide speed range from Mach 0.85 at 150 ft to low speed, as on the approach in full blow, and this meant that considerable effort, both on the ground and in the air, was needed before the system was perfected.

Although the designers Blackburn were faced with considerable challenges in the design of the B.103/NA.39 it is to their eternal credit that the first prototype aircraft was flown on 30 April 1958, less than five years after the issue of the requirement by the Admiralty. Right from the word go it was obvious that the B.103/NA.39, or, simply, NA.39 (the name Buccaneer was not adopted until August 1961) had tremendous potential and was only let down by a lack of power which meant that a critical situation could easily develop should an engine be lost during launch or recovery. This problem was eventually cured by the adoption of Rolls-Royce Spey bypass engines in the Buccaneer S.2 which offered 11,200 lb thrust and lower fuel consumption when in the cruise. As the mass flow of the Spey was greater than the Gyron Junior, the air intakes had to be enlarged and became oval in shape rather than circular.

Unfortunately this was to be the ultimate Buccaneer (the export S.50 for South Africa was a revised S.2 that was fitted with a retractable Bristol Siddeley BS.605 rocket motor for assisted take-off) as advanced versions proposed for the RAF remained as paper aeroplanes amid the turmoil of that service's strike requirements in the mid 1960s. Supersonics were the thing during that period and even when the TSR.2 was cancelled the RAF refused to consider a modified Buccaneer because even with reheated Spey engines and a thinner wing it would still have been a subsonic design. Add to this the political meddling of the new Labour government which favoured purchasing the General Dynamics F-111 as a TSR.2 replacement and the Buccaneer was pushed even further down the pecking order. By this time swing wings had become another 'must have' fashion accessory but in 1968 the F-111 order went the same way as the TSR.2 so that the RAF had little choice but to accept the standard Buccaneer S.2 as its principal strike aircraft. Had the RAF given the Buccaneer a chance (the fact that it was designed for the Royal Navy did not exactly help in this respect) it would have recognised the aircraft's qualities much sooner and an advanced variant might well have seen the light of day. With a revised and updated nav/attack system it would have been able to perform the same role as that intended for TSR.2, the fact that it would have been flown at low level at high subsonic instead of low supersonic speeds making very little difference to overall mission capability. As it was the RAF had to make do with the S.2 but once it had acquired first-hand experience, it soon became obvious that even the basic aircraft was one of the best strike/attack aircraft of its day.

CHAPTER TWO

Early Flight Testing

The first Blackburn NA.39 to be built was XK486 which was ready for its first flight in early 1958. The company airfield at Brough was too small for flight testing purposes but instead of choosing the nearby airfield at Holme-on-Spalding Moor, which offered a 6,000 ft runway that would have been more than adequate, the Ministry of Defence had reservations on its use and preferred either RAE Bedford or Boscombe Down, each of which had runways of over 9,000 ft. As a long road journey was involved to either location, Blackburn decided upon Bedford as it was the nearer of the two, but even this meant a trip of around 170 miles. After rebuilding, XK486 made its first flight at Bedford in the hands of Blackburn test pilot Derek Whitehead on 30 April 1958 with Bernard Watson, the head of flight test, in the rear seat. Flight testing was carried out from Bedford until 9 July 1958 when the aircraft was flown back to Home-on-Spalding Moor, the initial trials having convinced the Ministry that the safety of their precious prototype would not be compromised. By early September a total of 25 hours had been flown which was more than the minimum requirement for participation in the SBAC Farnborough Air Show, although the high level of security surrounding the aircraft at the time decreed that it should only take part in the flying display.

Four weeks after its appearance at Farnborough, XK486 was flown to Boscombe Down for the first preview assessment by pilots from A&AEE. This took place from 11-17 October 1958 and involved 8½ hours flying, during which time the aircraft's handling and performance characteristics were assessed, together with an evaluation of its operational potential in the strike role. The scope of these trials was restricted somewhat as the NA.39 was in the very early stages of development and a number of limitations had to be observed. These included a maximum altitude of 20,000 ft (this was due to a temporary limitation that had been imposed on the Gyron Junior engines), maximum 'g' +5 to -2.4, a maximum Mach number of 0.9 IMN and a maximum IAS of 450 knots. Stalling was prohibited under any condition of flight and minimum speeds for flight were 150 kts IAS in the clean configuration at 30,000 lb AUW, and 128 kts IAS with 45 degrees flap, 1 degrees aileron droop and Boundary Layer Control (BLC) at the same weight. The amount of aileron droop was restricted to 15 degrees for landing and 20 degrees during handling tests at a safe altitude (the design value was 30 degrees). The maximum speed for airbrake operation was 400 kts IAS and for the rotating bomb-door it was 350 kts IAS. As befitting its prototype status, XK486 had no provision for folding wings, a folding nose or a deck-landing arrester hook. No operational equipment had been installed and there was no provision for the carriage of external stores.

The all-up weight of the aircraft on arrival was 39,710 lb which approximated to that of a production aircraft with operational equipment, full internal fuel and a Red Beard tactical nuclear bomb. The fuel load was 11,820 lb and a proportioner system was used to control the remaining fuel so that the aircraft's centre of gravity (CG) was always within limits. The Gyron Junior engines were also at an early stage in their development and those fitted to XK486 during the preview were Phase 1A engines rated at 7,000 lb thrust, decreasing to 5,400 lb thrust when the aircraft was being flown with its BLC system operating.

The assessment of the cockpit was that it was roomy and comfortable and afforded an excellent view, however, there were a number of criticisms relating to the canopy. Although it was admitted that Blackburn had done well to come up with a clear, one-piece sliding canopy of such size, the sliding portion was heavy and as the rails ran upwards to the rear when in the normal ground attitude, opening by hand was virtually impossible. There was also no canopy control for the observer in the rear seat so if the pilot opened the canopy just past his own ejection seat, the observer was unable to leave his cockpit. It was also thought that jettisoning of the canopy with the aircraft stationary would result in the canopy falling back onto the cockpit with an obvious risk of injury to the crew. In addition, comments were made regarding the unprotected firing mechanism of the pilot's ejection seat. This presented a convenient hand-hold when climbing into either cockpit, and such a practice could well have led to an unfortunate crew member firing the seat unintentionally. The rudder pedals were also criticised as they had been designed with heel stirrups. These made accurate rudder applications difficult and problems were also experienced on the ground as excessive foot movement was needed to work the toe-operated brakes.

During taxiing trials it was discovered that the ground-idle setting of the throttle was 3,950 rpm which, even at maximum all-up weight, meant that the brakes had to be used continuously to control speed. However this was not too much of a hardship as the toe brakes were very powerful and progressive which made speed control relatively easy. Another aspect of taxiing which was commented upon was the nosewheel steering which was excessively sensitive over small angles. This characteristic, combined with a poorly positioned control, made it difficult to steer a straight course. Sharp turns could be made relatively easily although it was felt that the radius of turn, although adequate for an airfield, might not be sufficient for manoeuvring on a carrier deck.

The NA.39's oversensitive nosewheel steering was also apparent when lining up for take-off as it took some effort to get it to point straight down the runway. On releasing the brakes at full power the aircraft tended to develop a slight swing, although this could easily be checked by the nosewheel steering, before the rudder became effective at around 60 knots. Acceleration levels were relatively poor and the pilot had to wait before he could raise the nosewheel at 100-110 kts IAS. Without BLC a forward movement had to be made on the control column as the aircraft rotated to prevent an excessive attitude developing (with BLC switched on this situation was not evident). Despite the generally excellent view from the cockpit, it was found that attitude appreciation was not easy as there was relatively little forward reference. The aircraft was airborne at 140-150 kts IAS and climbed away with no trim changes. In calm air there was a certain amount of pilot-induced rocking of the wings, a feature which became more pronounced in rough air. After take-off, the undercarriage retracted rapidly with no change of trim. Raising the flaps and aileron droop, and switching off BLC, each produced a moderate nose-up trim change which was easily held and trimmed out.

In terms of longitudinal stability the NA.39 was statically stable over the whole speed range tested up to 0.9 IMN although it did appear that there was a reduction in stability as airspeed was increased above 400 kts IAS. No difficulty was experienced in accurate longitudinal trimming and no significant Mach number effects were apparent up to the limiting speed. In the landing configuration the aircraft exhibited excellent longitudinal stability and pilots had no difficulty in trimming or maintaining the correct approach speed. With regard to control during the approach a certain 'dead spot' was noted over small stick movements, but for larger movements adequate and effective control was achieved. Control forces in this configuration were moderately heavy and seemed to be slightly heavier in push than in pull. At speeds of 400 kts IAS and above at low altitude fore-and-aft control was becoming light and over-sensitive, although there was no sign of pitch-up. The longitudinal trimmer had two speeds, fast and slow, the former proving to be adequate throughout the speed range as tested, however the slow setting was too slow in operation for use at any speed.

Although stability was not a problem longitudinally, it was a different matter laterally and directionally. In calm air and with the yaw damper on, stability was satisfactory, although as already mentioned, there was a tendency for slight lateral rocking at low speeds (for the first preview assessment the

NA.39 was not fitted with a roll damper). If the air was slightly turbulent, however, there was a marked deterioration in lateral and directional stability throughout the speed range. This manifested itself in a continuous Dutch roll with a large roll/yaw ratio which could not be controlled within normal limits, even with the yaw damper in operation. This effect was at its worst in the landing configuration and attempts to control it were made more difficult by the very light and powerful rudder, together with the continuous and large aileron movements that were needed in turbulent air. This made the aircraft very tiring to fly. It also meant that pilots had great difficulty in lining the aircraft up accurately when on the approach.

Aileron effectiveness was considered to be just adequate for the landing approach when using 15 degrees of aileron droop with BLC. Control column movements were large and the associated forces were near the maximum desirable value. In contrast, at high speeds the lateral response for small aileron angles was great and all A&AEE pilots were of the opinion that, above 400 kts IAS, the control forces were becoming too light and the movements too small for a strike aircraft. The ailerons also produced some adverse yaw, particularly at low speed, and it was necessary to hold off bank during turns. This characteristic, together with the powerful, light and over-sensitive rudder, meant that it was very difficult to make accurate turns. The rudder control had to be used with great caution due to its considerable effectiveness and the low foot forces resulting from the interim feel system that was fitted to the aircraft at the time.

A number of Aerodrome Dummy Deck Landings (ADDLs) were flown with final approach being flown in the following configuration:

Undercarriage	Down
Flap	45 degrees (full)
Aileron droop	15 degrees
Tailplane flap	Up
Yaw damper	On
Airbrake	72 degrees (full)
BLC	On
Engine rpm	7,800-8,400

The normal circuit speed was 150-160 kts IAS depending on weight and this was flown at 500 ft with the engines set at 8,200-8,300 rpm. The optimum speed on final approach was considered to be 140 kts IAS at 36,000 lb AUW, reducing to 130 kts IAS at 31,000 lb. It was vital that these speeds be adhered to as a loss of even 3-4 knots led to a marked deterioration in speed control and it was possible to induce a high rate of descent so that the aircraft descended uncontrollably below the mirror path. This situation was made worse by the lack of available thrust from the Gyron Junior engines with BLC operating. In some cases during an ADDL approach it was necessary for the pilot to apply full power to arrest the descent and regain the desired approach path. As mentioned previously, Dutch rolling made life difficult for the pilot during approaches as he was forced to make continuous aileron applications. This was made even more tiring as the geometry of the control column required wrist movements rather than forearm movements. Once again, the rudder control was found to be too light and powerful to be used for accurate aileron/rudder control harmonisation during the ADDL pattern.

The view from the cockpit, forwards and downwards, was excellent, although the wide windscreen frames and local distortions meant that the pilot had to move his head if he was to keep the mirror in view as he was turning on to final approach. Touchdowns showed that the aircraft had little tendency to float or bounce. The NA.39's overshoot characteristics were also evaluated at a weight of 35,000 lb from 300 ft. The technique was to select full power and close the airbrakes and allow the speed to increase from 130 to 160 kts IAS. There was negligible height loss and the aircraft could be climbed away at a rate of 1,000 ft/min, engine response to throttle was good and the airbrakes closed rapidly. Single-engine ADDLs and overshoots were not attempted.

The buffet boundaries of the NA.39 were established in turns at 5,000 ft and 20,000 ft, although flight to the limits of lift coefficient was not possible in view of the restrictions to the flight envelope. No pitch-up or stick force lightening was experienced and there was no evidence of any pre-stall longitudinal instability. The onset of buffet in manoeuvring flight was well defined and it tended to become more marked with penetration. Pilot's impressions were that the order of buffet, even at the onset, would be such as to preclude appreciable penetration of the region of buffet by service pilots, especially under instrument conditions. Due to high levels of buffet, especially as Mach number was increased, the degree of manoeuvre was restricted, and it was felt that this might lead to severe limitations on the aircraft if no improvement was made. In addition to pilots not being able to make full use of the available lift boundary, it was felt that the buffet was severe enough to affect equipment serviceability.

One of the most striking aspects of the NA.39 design was the 'clam shell' airbrake which, when closed, formed the rear section of the fuselage. This was tested up to 400 kts IAS and was found to be quick in operation and produced excellent deceleration. A certain amount of buffet was experienced at all speeds, particularly towards the upper limit, but it was not excessive and it did not effect the aircraft's handling characteristics. The airbrakes were criticised, however, as the aircraft suffered from a nose-down trim change when they were extended. This became more noticeable with increase in speed, the trim change being deemed unacceptable at speeds in excess of 350 kts IAS as it was impossible to fly accurately when the airbrakes were in the process of being deployed. The rotating bomb-door was also tested and during its operation the aircraft rolled slowly through some 5 degrees to starboard with moderate buffet, however, once the door was fully open the buffet was much reduced. As the bomb door was closed there was also a slight roll to starboard which was easily countered by opposite aileron.

In the period after the issue of Specification M.148T, the role of the NA.39 was extended to include conventional weapon delivery in limited war conditions. Despite the fact that the performance limits that had been imposed meant that no typical operational sorties could be flown, either for simulated nuclear or conventional weapon delivery, the aircraft was flown at the maximum permissible test airspeed of 450 kts IAS for a considerable period. This gave pilots a good appreciation of the likely suitability of the aircraft in its operational role. The tactics that would probably be adopted for the nuclear and attack roles were quite different and the NA.39, not surprisingly, showed itself to be rather more suited to the former.

The nuclear type of attack was most likely to be carried out on a carefully pre-planned basis in which the full extent of the aircraft's performance capabilities would be employed. This would entail a climb after launch to the aircraft's best cruise height, followed by a cruise at altitude to approximately 250 nautical miles from the target. A descent would then be made so that the aircraft was at sea level at a point 100 nautical miles short of the target. The run to the target would be made at sea level (including five minutes at combat power) followed by a programmed manoeuvre for the delivery of the weapon. The return to the carrier would be along a similar flight profile. Throughout the trial the NA.39 had come in for adverse comment as regards its lack of acceleration, but it was felt that in this type of attack, such a deficiency would not be too much of a problem as the aircraft had a considerable distance to cover, including the descent from cruising altitude, in which to achieve its final speed for the attack phase. It was conceded, however, that at the higher airspeeds the forces felt through the control column were becoming too low for prolonged flight at high speed and low level. The early onset of buffet was also likely to affect adversely the delivery manoeuvre which was abbreviated as LABS (Low Altitude Bombing System) and involved the release or 'tossing' of the nuclear weapon as the aircraft pulled up into a half loop.

For the delivery of conventional weapons, certain assumptions were made by A&AEE as regards tactics. In a limited war situation it was considered that pre-planning of the flight profile would be impossible and that the aircraft would have to fly at low level to stay clear of ground defences. It was also thought that airspeed would have to be reduced to ensure good navigation and target identification. When the position of the target had been ascertained a climb would have to be made at some point so that the attack could be delivered in a dive. For this type of attack to be carried out successfully the strike aircraft would have to be extremely flexible, particularly in its ability to accelerate and decelerate quickly. Although the NA.39 could certainly slow down quickly enough as a result of its powerful airbrakes, it was a different matter in terms of acceleration, and when operating at low level no benefit could be made by converting height into speed. There was also no immediate prospect of increased engine thrust as the early development Phase 1A engines, as fitted to XK486 for the first preview, produced as much thrust as the ultimate production standard. In the words of A&AEE – 'serious doubts exist as to there being sufficient margin of thrust available for the aircraft to carry out efficiently its limited war role in the 1960+ era. Every effort should be made to provide appreciably more available engine thrust in the combat condition.'

Although A&AEE had made several reservations as regards performance and handling, the overall impression of the NA.39 was favourable and it was recognised that many of the aspects that they had criticised were being addressed by Blackburn in their ongoing development programme. After the first preview XK486 was returned to Holme-on-Spalding Moor and by the end of the year it had been joined by XK487 and XK488. Various aerodynamic modifications were made in an attempt to cure the handling deficiencies identified at Boscombe Down and changes were also made to the controls. By the spring of 1959 these had all been embodied and XK486 was returned to A&AEE for a second preview assessment which was carried out from 23-28 April.

The main changes to XK486 were as follows. To improve the aircraft's buffet boundary rectangular vortex generators were fitted on the upper surface of the wing from 50 per cent of the semi-span to the tip. There were thirty generators each side at 4 in spacing, the inboard six being at 10 per cent local chord and the remainder tapered to 20 per cent local chord at the tip. The wing leading edge also had increased camber, giving effectively a flat undersurface, and small radius (leading edge BLC was temporarily deleted on this trial installation). The unwanted trim change on operation of the airbrakes had led to a redesign of the top strake on each half of the airbrake which was aligned vertically instead of at 45 degrees to the vertical. There was also a very small increase in area. Damping was now provided for all three axes and the rudder feel force for full movement was increased from 50 lb to 94 lb to overcome the over-sensitive nature of the rudder as noted during the first preview. The engines were still Phase 1A Gyron Juniors but engine idling rpm had been increased to 4,400 to improve high altitude engine handling. The speed limitation was still 450 kts IAS, but the maximum permissible altitude had been raised to 37,000 ft and pilots were allowed to manoeuvre up to a maximum accelerometer reading of +6.5g. The take-off weight was now 39,880 lb.

The first trial flights to be undertaken involved buffet boundaries and tests were made at 4,000 ft, 20,000 ft and 37,000 ft to establish the manoeuvre boundary at the onset of buffet. During the first preview the commencement of buffet was considered to be severe enough to preclude appreciable penetration, however, the second set of trials showed a notable improvement and although the onset of buffet was still well marked, the levels were now acceptable. Measurements showed that there was a substantial increase in usable lift coefficient at the higher Mach numbers, so that at 0.9 TMN, the improvement was around 60 per cent. The results of these trials had an important bearing on the delivery manoeuvre that would be used for toss bombing. This involved a 5g pull up from sea level at 625 kts TAS and it had been calculated that in the previous case the aircraft would be in buffet at this speed at only 4.8g. As the NA.39 was now much improved in this respect a fresh set of calculations had to be made and these showed that the available 'g' at sea level would, in fact, be in excess of the design limit of 8g. No detailed investigation was made of conditions beyond the onset of buffet, but it was noticed that the aircraft tended to drop a wing in the direction of the turn if 'g' levels were increased.

Further testing was aimed at seeing whether or not the nose-down trim change on extending the airbrake had been eradicated by its revised design. On opening the airbrakes fully with the control column released, there was no trim change for about the first 60 degrees of opening. Thereafter, up to the fully open position of 72 degrees there was a very slight nose down followed by a nose-up trim change which could be overcome by forward stick movement equivalent to ½ degree tailplane movement. This compared favourably with the marked nose-down trim change of 2.2 degrees with the original strakes. The improvement was described as 'praiseworthy', and it was also noted that this had been brought about with no noticeable increase in buffet.

Although much progress had been achieved with the handling characteristics of the NA.39, the news was less good when it came to lateral and directional stability, even though the aircraft was now fitted with a roll damper. In the first preview pronounced Dutch rolling had occurred in any form of turbulence, particularly in the deck-landing configuration. On one occasion marked Dutch rolling was experienced at altitude. The yaw and roll dampers had been switched off at 35,000 ft as it was thought that they may have been causing a slight tremor which was being experienced at the time. The pilot stated that he was unable to control the Dutch roll that had been set up and it seemed to him that any attempt to correct it only made the oscillation worse.

The tests that were carried out in the approach configuration only served to reinforce what was already known about the aircraft's poor level of lateral and directional stability and improvements were called for as a matter of the highest priority. It was known that the manufacturers were intending to test a yaw damper having increased authority, but it was felt that the characteristics of the NA.39 without autostabilisation, particularly on the approach, were such as to make it essential that the dampers be duplicated. Deliberate wing drops of about 30 degrees were made on the approach with aileron droop set to 15 or 20 degrees. In each case corrective aileron took about 1¹/₂ seconds to raise the wing. This was considered to be satisfactory, although constant corrections of this nature in turbulent conditions would be quite tiring for the pilot. In its conclusion to the second preview, A&AEE welcomed the marked progress that had been made in the previous six months, but the lack of improvement in terms of lateral and directional stability was still a cause for concern, and required urgent development work.

Catapult and Initial Deck Trials

The initial catapulting trials of the NA.39 were carried out from the raised artificial deck catapult at RAE Bedford from 3-20 July 1959. These were to ascertain the aircraft's handling characteristics during launching and to determine the minimum launching speeds at various all-up weights. The aircraft used was XK489, the fourth prototype, which had been flown for the first time on 28 January 1959. It was still in good condition by the time it arrived at Bedford, the blowing slots were positioned as for production aircraft, although the amount of blow was less. The engines had been modified to run on varying fuels, particularly AVCAT, and the trials were mostly carried out with this type of fuel [AVCAT or JP-5 is a jet fuel with a high flash point and is most suitable for use on aircraft carriers where the risk of fire is particularly great]. Weather during the trial period was good with only slight turbulence and winds varying from calm to 20 knots. All flights were made with a crew of two and the launches were made with 30 degrees flap, 20 degrees aileron droop and 20 degrees of up tailplane flap, with blow on.

The first launch was made at 33,395 lb AUW at a true end speed of 147 knots (the acceleration was 4.3g). It was during this launch that the first sign of pitch-up was encountered. About half way down the launch the nose suddenly rose by about 4 degrees and as the aircraft left the end of the 'deck', forward stick was required to lower the angle of incidence. The second launch at this weight was made at 151 knots and the pilot tried to anticipate the pitch-up tendency by holding on forward stick. This had no effect until the aircraft left the end when a violent pitch-down commenced. This was checked with back stick and the fly away was level with a slight amount of pitch oscillation. This particular characteristic was to be seen to a greater or lesser extent throughout the trial at all the varying speeds and weights that were attempted.

Launching speeds were lowered progressively until the final launch which was made at a speed of only 108 knots. As speeds were reduced there was a general deterioration in the level of controllability, the ailerons in particular being poor in response. The aircraft tended to fly away in a nose-high attitude and there was some lateral wallowing and slight airframe buffet. Acceleration was rather slow, but was considered to be acceptable nonetheless. The same launch speed was attempted at the higher weight of 37,304 lb. On this occasion the pilot held the stick in the half back position in an attempt to arrest the initial sink off the end of the catapult, but this was insufficient to prevent the aircraft from touching the runway after approximately 500-600 yards. Further back stick was used and the aircraft finally got airborne in a very nose-high attitude.

The highest launch weight that was flown during the Bedford trials was 40,332 lb and the lowest end speed attempted at this weight was 116 knots. To achieve this increased weight, ballast was carried in the bomb bay which also served to keep the CG within the aft limit. The normal CG shift with the consumption of fuel was forwards. Perhaps not surprisingly at the higher weights, the aircraft lost height off the end of the catapult, the pilot initially using half back stick in an attempt to recover. This only had a partial effect, however, and the stick had to be moved further back to the three-quarter position before the sink was stopped. The aircraft then pitched up of its own accord to about 17 degrees incidence, although it did so in a fairly gentle manner which could be controlled by easing the control column into the central position and then back again. From all of this it was concluded that the minimum safe launching speed at a typical all-up weight of 40,000 lb was 120 kts TAS.

The overall conclusions of the catapult trials were that the launch should be made with the control column held central and that 0 degrees tailplane trim should be used except for launches below 33,000 lb, when some negative trim of up to –4 degrees was necessary. It was also recommended that pilots should be warned of the pitch-up tendency down the catapult. From the pilot's point of view this behaviour was somewhat disconcerting on first experience and was put down to the high forward CG position which caused a rotating moment under linear acceleration. This effect was found to be more pronounced than on the Scimitar due to the shorter base between the main wheels and tail strut, the latter also being rather softer than on the Supermarine aircraft. On the occasions that the NA.39 pitched up, the elevator was immediately effective at reducing the angle of incidence.

The initial deck landing trials with the NA.39 at sea were due to have taken place at the end of 1959 but these unfortunately had to be put back to early the following year following the loss of XK490 on 12 October (see Chapter Eleven). The aircraft involved in the trials were XK489 and XK523 and these were flown from HMS *Victorious* in the English Channel. Both aircraft were fully navalised with folding outer-wings and nose section, together with an arrester hook, tail skid and catapult hooks. The controls had also been modified with revised aileron gearing to improve the aircraft's lateral characteristics at low speeds and reduced friction in the longitudinal control circuit. An Elliott three-axis autostabiliser was fitted to both aircraft and in addition XK489 was fitted with a Blackburn (Hobson) autostabiliser operating on the rudder only. This installation was intended as a standby system to be used in the event of failure of the unduplicated Elliott system. A full Boundary Layer Control system was fitted with blowing over the wing leading edge, flaps and ailerons, and also the under-surface of the tailplane leading edge, using a 9 per cent bleed from the engine compressors. The wing flap, aileron droop and tailplane flap configuration used for catapult launching was 30/20/20 with airbrakes in and BLC on. For ADDLs and deck landing, the configuration adopted was 45/25/20 with full airbrake (72 degrees) and BLC on (the tailplane flap was set at a negative angle to the airflow but for clarity has been recorded here, and throughout the book, without the minus prefix).

Prior to the trials that took place aboard HMS *Victorious* a series of ADDLs were flown at Boscombe Down. These were carried out using XK489 (XK523 was still at Holme-on-Spalding Moor having been delayed due to bad weather), the purpose being to establish handling characteristics, touchdown speeds and to provide pilots with the necessary practice before the carrier trials got under way. By now the recommended aileron droop angle when landing had gone up to 25 degrees and as a result the manufacturers had proposed a reduction in the nominal approach speed of 2-3 kts IAS, however, a deterioration in handling characteristics was noted when these lower approach speeds were used. In particular, large throttle movements were sometimes necessary to check a tendency to sink and the twin goals of accurate speed control and an accurate approach were difficult to attain, especially in turbulent conditions. When using an aileron droop setting of 25 degrees the approach was flown at a speed of 125 kts IAS at 30,000 lb AUW with an increase of 2 kts IAS for every 1,000 lb above this weight.

General handling on deck was, once again, found to be difficult due to the nose-wheel steering being over sensitive at small angles. This made accurate steering almost impossible, particularly when using the small corrections that were necessary when lining up on the catapult. A total of thirty-one launches were made during the deck trials (fourteen on XK523 and seventeen on XK489) at weights varying from 32,170 lb to 37,470 lb. Due to adverse weather conditions and lack of time it was not possible to determine the minimum launching speeds, or carry out launches at the maximum permissible weight of 40,000 lb. At the higher launching speeds used there was no necessity to rotate the aircraft after leaving the catapult and only a small change of incidence was needed at the lower launch speeds. For the majority of launches the undercarriage was left down and in this condition the level of acceleration on becoming airborne was very slow, but at no time did any sink occur. It was hoped that with more representative engines (the Gyron

Juniors fitted to XK489 and XK523 were still early development Phase 1A engines) there would be increased thrust with BLC on so that acceleration would be acceptable up to the estimated maximum take-off weight of 41,000 lb for production aircraft.

During approaches and deck landings it was apparent that many of the criticisms that had been made of the NA.39 during the previews had been acted upon and the problems had either been eliminated or reduced to an acceptable level. In the approach configuration with the Elliott autostabiliser system operating on the rudder and ailerons the Dutch rolling tendencies that had previously been experienced were markedly reduced even in the moderately turbulent conditions that prevailed during much of the trial. The improvement was such that this aspect of the aircraft's handling was no longer considered a problem. The excellent results achieved with the Elliott system were unfortunately not repeated with the back-up Blackburn (Hobson) autostabiliser. Using this installation the aircraft was difficult to turn when in the approach configuration, even when applying large rudder angles, and there was also the return of Dutch rolling which could easily be induced with any lateral control correction, however small. For this reason the Blackburn (Hobson) autostabiliser was considered to be inadequate even as a back-up system.

Another significant improvement was the introduction of increased aileron gearing which resulted in better lateral control characteristics during the approach. This was not a complete fix, however, as response for small stick movements was still not good and the control forces were also considered to be rather heavy. The difficulties that had been experienced in lining up the aircraft accurately, first noticed during ADDLs, were considerably increased during actual deck landings due to turbulence in the ship's wake and the apparent inability of the ship to maintain a steady heading. Although pilots had no difficulty in applying control corrections, the aircraft's inertia meant that response was slow. This problem was particularly noticeable during the last 3-4 seconds of the approach with great concentration being needed on the part of the pilot to stay on the centre line. On occasions very large lateral and directional control movements were required at a very late stage in the approach to ensure an accurate touchdown. Although the weather conditions experienced during the deck landing trials were not ideal, they were by no means severe. All of the pilots who took part in the trial were highly experienced, and the fact that they had their hands full with the NA.39 on final approach, did not bode well for the future unless further improvements could be made to the aircraft's handling.

It was a similar story longitudinally as the reduced friction in the elevator circuit resulted in an improvement, however, the control was still considered to be too heavy with some 'dead' stick movement for small movements about the trimmed position. Pilots found it difficult to synchronise throttle and tailplane movements when height corrections were needed to return to the correct glide path. For example, if the aircraft was below the mirror path the application of more power together with a rearward stick movement inevitably resulted in an increase in airspeed before any appreciable change in the approach path occurred. If, however, the pilot chose to use tailplane only in the same circumstances the airspeed reduced immediately, well before the glide path was regained. Accurate speed control was equally as difficult if the aircraft was above the mirror path.

Although the development effort being put in to the NA.39 was clearly making progress, there was still some way to go if the pilots' task during carrier landings was to be reduced. This was an important issue as the aircraft would have to be flown in service in conditions worse than those prevalent during the trial, by pilots with much less experience. During the trial the vertical velocities on touchdown were also generally excessive and it was hoped that further improvements in the control system would reduce these to more acceptable levels.

The following are extracts from the detailed flight reports of one of the pilots who took part in the deck trials. These give a good indication of what it was like to land a combat aircraft on an aircraft carrier, together with the particular characteristics of the NA.39:

Deck handling assessment

At all times during this trial the aircraft was manned on deck and except in very strong conditions of wind, no difficulty was experienced. When entering the cockpit under conditions of strong wind and deck movement it was found that the present entrance ladder was bulky to grip and gave no support when transferring from the ladder to the cockpit; this deficiency was also most apparent when leaving the cockpit in a confined space such as FLY1.

Initially, taxiing on deck and onto the catapult was attempted using a combination of brake and nose-wheel steer. Although a mislead never occurred, the pilot found it most difficult to follow the director's instructions at the speed either he or the director would have desired using this technique. Subsequently the pilot used only braking power for manoeuvring on deck and although this required more use of engine power and rather heavy use of the brakes, much more precise and earlier response to director's signals was achieved. Launches were made from both the port and starboard catapults and while this technique of using brakes only proved adequate, it was considered that the task might well be made easier if more authority was available on the nose wheel steer. This was particularly true in the case of the starboard catapult where small radius turns were required.

Catapult launching assessment

The attitude on the catapult was comfortable, and it was not found necessary to alter the aircraft's incidence after launching at these speeds in order to climb away or achieve the desired circuit speed. Acceleration along the catapult was smooth, and apart from a slight tendency for the pilot to move forward at about the three-quarter catapult travel point, no unusual characteristics were noted. The aircraft's acceleration after launching at these end speeds, while poor when compared with a Sea Vixen, was more than adequate and at no time did the pilot feel he was short of airspeed. End speeds were lowered progressively as experience was gained; the lowest end speed achieved was of the order of 116 knots. It was most noticeable that when the IAS off the catapult was less than 125 knots, the aircraft took a marked period of time at full power to reach the desired 150 knots for the initial climb away. On all launches the undercarriage was left extended and no doubt a more rapid acceleration would be achieved when selecting wheels up after launching. On the one occasion when the end speed was 116 knots, the first IAS reading the pilot saw was 118 knots and he was very conscious of reducing attitude in order to build up speed.

Deck landing assessment

The turn in from the downwind leg was made at a point approximately abreast the mirror, indicated height 600 ft, ASI 150 knots and airbrakes extended to the 60 degree position, the final 12 degrees of airbrakes being used on the final approach to make late adjustment to the final approach speed. Provided height was maintained on the initial part of the turn in from downwind, the mirror was picked up at approximately the 90 degree position although it was not always possible to identify the source light at this point, there being a marked lack of definition particularly when the ship was steaming down sun. Speed was reduced progressively from the turn-in point, aiming to be lined up and in the mirror at the Datum speed + 5 knots at a point approximately 2,000 yards astern at an indicated height of 300 ft. This technique was employed on every approach and no difficulty was experienced up to this stage of the approach.

Once this aircraft was lined up, no difficulty was experienced in flying the glide path provided the ship maintained a steady heading. The airspeed was decayed slowly to be at the optimum over the round down; approximately 8,000 RPM per engine and a tailplane trim setting of -5 degrees were used during the final approach and these conditions gave a steady glide path under ideal conditions. Having once established the line up under steady deck conditions, only small control movements were required to bring the aircraft onto the deck with the nose wheel on the centre line.

It was considered that only on the first sortie could the conditions of deck movement be described as ideal and it was most noticeable during subsequent approaches and landings that it was extremely difficult to keep the aircraft lined up with the ship's centre line and at the same time maintain a centre mirror, when there was any degree of ship movement. On several occasions some very large aileron deflections were needed at a very late stage of the approach to correct the line, due either to ship movement or turbulence in the ship's wake. These large aileron deflections produced a very rapid rate of roll but not a proportional amount of turn, and it was therefore necessary to use much more rudder than is customary in conventional aircraft.

On one sortie three successive bolters were made due to the aircraft bouncing clear of the wires after touchdown short of No.1 wire. The pilot was of the opinion on each occasion that a satisfactory approach had been carried out and the flight observer confirmed that the touchdown speed was within +/- 1 knot of the desired optimum. On each occasion the pilot's last mirror indication had been central, but it should be pointed out that a considerable amount of lateral correction was required during these approaches, and this no doubt divided the pilot's attention more than usual between glide path and line up. Adequate power was available to carry out the bolter, the aircraft accelerated and climbed immediately full power was applied and the airbrake selected closed.

On several occasions during the approach to land the pilot noticed a very slight heavying of the port wing as the aircraft flew into the ship's wake. Approximately 150-200 yards short of the round down it was also noticed that a standing wave caused the aircraft to balloon above the glide path, but provided this movement was arrested immediately by a positive forward stick movement, no embarrassment ensued. The slightest delay in correction entailed very large fore-and-aft stick movements with the risk of touching down at a much higher vertical velocity than was desirable.

A three degree mirror angle was used during the whole trial and apart from the feeling that the aircraft was too close to the round down when flying a centre mirror, no other obvious deficiencies were noticed. The view throughout the final approach was good, but if the pilot did not fly into the centre line from the starboard side it was necessary to move the head to the right in order to keep the mirror in view. After the initial turn in from the down-wind leg it was only possible to keep the ship in view by very large deflections of the head, and it was not until 45 degrees of the turn had been completed that the ship could be kept in view through the front quarter panel without undue straining.

Lateral and Directional Characteristics
As during ADDLs no Dutch rolling characteristic was present, even in the turbulence encountered in the ship's wake. Any rapid lateral displacement was impossible. Although initial lining up was fairly straightforward, if subsequent aircraft drift or ship wander necessitated a correction, the time and concentration required were at the expense of the other variables, but particularly mirror path. The effort and concentration involved were not so much in readily achieving the desired bank angle for the correction, but in the delay involved in the aircraft subsequently moving sideways in space. Thus, the rolling power of the aileron and the stick movement required did not appear unreasonable for the type of aircraft, although the control was slightly heavy. Only normal co-ordinated rudder movements were made during azimuth corrections, and again time was not available to investigate the effect of increased rudder angles. However, no slip or skid was apparent to the pilot during the correction.

Longitudinal Characteristics
As in ADDLs, the delay in response to the fore-and-aft control movements deemed expedient in this aircraft made for difficulty in correction to the mirror path. This again was very pronounced when on being low in the mirror, attempts at regaining the correct path by means of tailplane and throttle resulted inevitably in an increase in airspeed and a delayed return to the optimum mirror path. Thus relatively greater time and concentration were required in this aircraft to carry out height corrections. From the downwind leg to arresting, a slight push force was held to assist in carrying out the turn in and subsequent decay of airspeed. This assisted in reducing both the weight and the amplitude of control required, particularly in the turn in where it was relatively easy to lose height.

Decaying airspeed on the final approach and maintenance of the optimum approach airspeed was fairly straightforward. However, any corrections required were not easy to make accurately with the large throttle movements required and the delay in aircraft response. On approaching the round down there was the usual flicker of airspeed associated with turbulence; this was ignored and no throttle corrections applied. View of the carrier during the turn in was obscured by the port windscreen pillar, and some head movement was required. Having lined up, the view of the deck was excellent throughout.

Normally the 'no cut' technique was used, and the aircraft flown on to the deck with the tailplane control held fixed. On one occasion, however, with the deck pitching away from the aircraft path, the rate of descent appeared high and almost full back-stick was applied just before touchdown. This had no apparent effect in reducing the vertical velocity. On occasions when the hook picked up a wire before the main wheels touched, the arresting was smooth, with no tendency to bounce or peck. However, when touchdown occurred before hook engagement, a bounce inevitably developed. The aircraft would rotate on to its nose wheel and then bounce into the air off all three wheels. Although on no occasion did this result in missing all the wires, the subsequent arresting was uncomfortable.

Bolting

On one occasion owing to a late correction in azimuth, a high mirror path was flown at the later stages and the aircraft touched down forward of the last wire without engagement. The resulting bolter was easy and straightforward with no tendency to sink. However, owing to the characteristic of the aircraft pitching onto its nose wheel on touchdown, a slight rotation was necessary on leaving the angled deck.

The Buccaneer S.1 Described

T
he following is taken from the aircraft servicing manual for the Buccaneer S.1 and serves to describe the basic structural elements of the design and the various systems that were incorporated throughout the structure.

The Buccaneer S.1 aircraft is a low level, long-range strike aircraft powered by two axial turbojet engines designed for service in the Royal Navy. Two crew members are carried, pilot and observer, seated in tandem in a cabin which can be pressurised for high-altitude flight. Moderately swept, blended-kink main planes, a high set all-moving tailplane and a cone-shaped rear fuselage extension (which opens clamshell fashion to serve as an airbrake) form distinctive features. A capacious bay, located in the lower half of the centre fuselage, is enclosed by a large door upon which weapons and other stores are mounted. The door rotates through 180 degrees to the open position, exposing the stores and thus providing a launching or dropping platform. Underwing stores can be carried on pylons fitted to both the inner and outer planes.

For carrier operations an arresting hook, tailskid, hold-back gear and two assisted take-off hooks are fitted in their conventional positions on the fuselage; these items retract when not in use. The main planes incorporate a power-operated, single-break folding mechanism between the inner and outer planes, folding upwards and inwards over the centre fuselage. The fuselage nose cone is folded rearwards to reduce the length of the aircraft for storage.

During manufacture, the fuselage structure is built in the following three main sections

1. Nose and cabin
2. Centre fuselage, including engine and jet pipe nacelles
3. Rear fuselage

On final assembly, the sections are joined together to form a single unit.

The basic cabin structure consists of front and rear pressure bulkheads (spanned at the top by two longerons), vertical frames and longitudinal stringers. A sliding one-piece canopy – which can be jettisoned in an emergency – surmounts the structure. Extending between the bulkheads is a pressure floor on which the crew members' ejection seats and equipment are installed. Occupying the space below the floor is a housing for the nose-wheel unit.

In the centre fuselage, which is the main load bearing structure, are three compartments arranged as follows:

1. An upper compartment, extending the length of the section, which is divided into eight internal fuel tanks
2. Two lower compartments, the forward one of which is divided into two small equipment bays (housing engine-driven gearboxes, accessories, piping and other services), and the large rear one forming the bomb bay.

At each extremity of the section is a bulkhead, between which are port and starboard longerons which run through the bomb and accessories bays. The fuel tank floor forms the roof for both lower bays, these compartments are separated by a substantial bulkhead. Reinforced frames are provided for the auxiliary, front and rear spar attachments. Structurally, the rear fuselage is orthodox, employing vertical and rearward-inclined frames, the latter coinciding with the fin support structure. A large bay is formed within the section and accommodates radio and electrical equipment. Access is gained through a hatch positioned just forward of the housing for the arresting gear.

Each main plane is attached to the centre fuselage section at three points – the auxiliary, the front and rear spars. When assembled, the inner plane is classified as part of the centre fuselage and is not normally dismantled; small-span, plain flaps are hinged to the trailing edge. The outer plane is of integral, stressed-skin construction with an aileron, hinged to the trailing edge, extending the full span. The root ends of the outer plane spars are machined to form the hinge and latch fittings. Attachment fittings for wing pylons are provided on the inner and outer planes.

The tail unit comprises a large fin which is surmounted by an all-moving tailplane. A conventional rudder is hinged to the rear of the fin, while a trimming flap is hinged to the trailing edge of the tailplane. This flap is used in conjunction with an aileron droop mechanism and a blowing (Boundary Layer Control) system for take-off and landing. The alighting gear is hydraulically operated and comprises two undercarriage units which retract inwards into recesses formed in the inner wings and engine nacelles, and a steerable nose-wheel unit, which retracts rearwards into a bay beneath the cabin floor. A liquid-spring shock absorber strut is fitted to each unit and hydraulically operated disc brakes, with anti-skid units, are fitted to the main wheels.

The main flying control surfaces are controlled by an orthodox control column and rudder pedals, operation being effected by hydraulically powered control units. Each power unit, one for each aileron, one for the rudder and one for the tailplane, is fully duplicated by a tandem ram served by two independent hydraulic systems. The wing flaps and airbrakes are also hydraulically operated but are served by a different hydraulic system, provision is made, however, for emergency operation. Electrical actuators are connected to the three main control circuits to enable trimming to be effected. A single switch controls two electrical actuators which move the aileron droop mechanism and tailplane trimming flap, both surfaces functioning at a synchronised rate. Hydraulically operated feel units, controlled by pitot/static pressure, give simulated feel to the power operated rudder and tailplane controls in relation to height and forward speed, this system is powered by the starboard flying controls hydraulic system.

Power is derived from two de Havilland Gyron Junior engines which are installed one on each side of the fuselage centre section. Each mounting comprises two trunnions located in spherical bearings with two rear attachment points, suspended from the top of the auxiliary spar ring. From each engine a universal drive shaft projects to the accessories bay, where it is coupled to a gearbox mounted on the rear face of the accessories bay dividing bulkhead, each gearbox driving identical units.

A tapping from an air bleed muff surrounding the rear of each engine combustion chamber casing supplies air pressure for the air bleed system. The system serves the blowing (Boundary Layer Control) system, fuel system (for tank pressurisation, negative-g recuperators and fuel/no-air valves), radio bay air conditioning, turbo alternator drive, windscreen clearance and hydraulic fluid reservoir pressurisation. A tapping at the base of each engine entry casing supplies air pressure for the cabin air conditioning and pressurisation, windscreen de-misting, windscreen wash, anti-g suits, ventilated suit, accessories bay cooling, radome conditioning and pressurisation systems. A further tapping at the top of each engine entry casing supplies air for the engine anti-icing system.

Fuel is carried in eight internal tanks built into the upper compartment of the centre fuselage and coupled in pairs for supply purposes. Four of the tanks (master tanks) feed fuel direct to the engines, the other four serving as slave tanks to the master tanks. Fuel is transferred by air pressure from the slave tanks to replenish the master tanks as the fuel is consumed. Long Range slipper tanks may be fitted to the inner wing-pylon attachments, fuel from these tanks being transferred by air pressure as fuel is used from the fuselage tanks. A single pressure-refuelling coupling is provided for refuelling and defuelling on the ground, while on pre-Mod 881 aircraft a retractable Flight

Refuelling probe is situated in the nose of the aircraft. On post-Mod 881 aircraft, the retractable Flight Refuelling probe is deleted, although provision is still made for the fitment of a fixed probe where required.

From the tanks, fuel is supplied through hydraulically driven flow proportioners, flowmeter transmitters and low pressure cocks to the engines. An inter-tank transfer system and cross-feed systems controlled by electrically activated cocks, together with pneumatically operated negative-g recuperators, ensure that a fuel supply is always available, even when normal feed conditions cannot be maintained. Four electrically operated jettison valves allow fuel from all the fuselage tanks to be discharged through a single outlet on the underside of the rear fuselage.

Power for the two flying control hydraulic systems is supplied by two pumps, one on each engine driven gearbox. Each pump serves one half of each of the four powered control units so that, in the event of failure of either engine or pump, the flying controls remain operative. Two more pumps, one on each gearbox, provide power for the general services hydraulic system. The general services are,

1. Alighting gear
2. Nose wheel steering
3. Wheel brakes
4. Wing flaps
5. Bomb door
6. Airbrakes
7. Flight Refuelling probe (pre-Mod 881 only)
8. Wing fold mechanism
9. Arresting hook
10. Retractable tail skid
11. Fuel flow proportioners

The system can, under certain emergency conditions, supply hydraulic pressure to one of the two flying controls hydraulic systems. A windscreen wiper, operated by an independent hydraulic system powered by two electrically driven pumps is also incorporated.

Power for the 28v d.c. electrical system is provided by two 6kw generators mounted on separate engine driven gearboxes in the accessories bay. Regulation of the generators' output is achieved by two voltage regulators. Two 24v 25 amp-hour batteries are installed, one of them being used as an emergency source of supply. The d.c. electrical services derive their power from a common busbar located on the port and starboard control panels which are situated in the accessories bay. Most of the wiring is carried out in Nyvia cable, its coding being based on the SBAC system.

The a.c. power supplies for the electrically-operated instruments, radio, radar and navigation equipment is provided by an air turbine alternator located in the radio bay and driven by air pressure tapped from the air bleed system; a.c. power for emergency use is supplied by a Type 107 inverter. For de-icing purposes, a gold film element is sandwiched between the glass laminates of the windscreen, functioning with power drawn from the a.c. supplies.

Pitot and static pressure for the air-operated instruments are obtained from a pressure head positioned on the leading edge of the port outer plane. The standby instruments and hydraulic feel systems are supplied with pitot pressure from a pressure head beneath the nose fuselage, true static being sensed by two static vents, one on each side of the folding nose.

The majority of the radio and electronic equipment is housed in the radio bay located in the rear fuselage. Communications is by UHF and HF radio, the intercom system forming an integral part of these two installations. A podded pressurised unit in the nose houses the scanner of a search radar installation, the nose cone being formed into a radome manufactured from resin-bonded glasscloth. The integrated instruments, automatic pilot and electronic equipment combine with the radio and radar systems to form a control and navigational system and provide a weapon system for attack.

Martin Baker Type 4 MS or MSA ejection seats are fitted, each seat complete with an electrically driven raising and lowering mechanism; a Mk8C emergency oxygen set and a Martin Baker multi-service personal equipment connector, cater for the crew members' services. Post Mod 631 aircraft incorporate an underwater escape system, operated automatically or manually, which ejects the crew at a much reduced velocity by means of compressed air. On pre Mod 917 aircraft, two 3½ litre containers, situated in the radome bay, form independent sources for two identical liquid oxygen systems which supply oxygen to the crew via Mk.17 regulators. These systems merge at a two-way check valve solely to provide emergency supplies if one system fails. On post Mod 917 aircraft, a liquid oxygen package unit, including a single 10 litre container, replaces the two existing containers and supplies both the pilot and observer via a single delivery line which branches in the cabin to each regulator.

CHAPTER FIVE

Intensive Flying Trials
RNAS Lossiemouth

With the issue of the CA Release for the Buccaneer S.1 in March 1961 the Royal Navy was at last able to make final preparations for the new aircraft to enter service. The first unit to fly the Buccaneer was No.700Z Flight which was set up to conduct a series of intensive flying trials and was commanded by Lieutenant-Commander Alan J. 'Spiv' Leahy DSC. The base chosen for these operations was RNAS Lossiemouth which boasted an excellent weather record and also offered relatively clear airspace with good low flying areas nearby.

Lieutenant Commander Leahy was an extremely experienced Royal Navy pilot having joined in 1943 as a Naval Airman 2nd Class. He was trained by the US Navy and went on to fly the Vought F4U Corsair before qualifying as an Air Weapons Officer. In 1953 he was awarded the DSC for operations over Korea flying Sea Furies of 801 Squadron from HMS *Glory*. He later commanded 738 Squadron on Sea Hawks and was the leader of the all red Royal Navy Sea Hawk aerobatic team of five aircraft that appeared at the 1957 Farnborough Air Show. Although the arrival of the Buccaneer was eagerly anticipated Alan Leahy had to wait another three months before he was able to fly one as he recalls,

> We formed 700Z Flight, the Buccaneer Intensive Flying Trials Unit (IFTU), at RNAS Lossiemouth (HMS *Fulmar*) on 7 March 1961. Lieutenant-Commander Derek Whitehead, the Chief Test Pilot of the Blackburn Aircraft Company, flew the first Buccaneer up to Lossiemouth for the ceremony. Unfortunately directly after the ceremony he took the aircraft back to Holme-on-Spalding Moor in order that the aircraft could continue its test flying programme. That left the Flight with one Sea Hawk, two Meteors, and three Hunter T.7s. However, what we were also left with was the authority to practice low level navigation all over the North and West of Scotland. Using the Meteors and the Hunters we were able to give our observers a foretaste of what was to come. Only one pilot, Lieutenant-Commander Ted

Anson, had already flown the Buccaneer as he had trained at the Empire Test Pilots School (then at Farnborough) and had been appointed to Blackburn Aircraft to assist with the development flying. The other pilots came to 700Z Flight from flying Scimitars, Hunters, Sea Vixens, and the Douglas A-4D Skyhawk. The observers came from the Sea Vixen, AEW Gannet and the ASW Wessex and they were all looking forward to a place in the sun in the back of the Buccaneer where they could actually see where they were going.

It was not until the end of June 1961 that three pilots were to be able to fly the Buccaneer when we went to Boscombe Down to carry out our first solos under the close supervision of 'C' Squadron, the Naval Test Squadron. I was the only pilot of the three who had actually flown an aircraft made by the Blackburn Aircraft Company and that was the Firebrand, a single-seat torpedo-strike fighter. This was a pig's ear of an aeroplane and I wondered what we were about to experience. After a thorough briefing, the 'C' Squadron observer, Lieutenant C. Walsh, and I started the aircraft, which was to be the first one we were due to get, and started to taxi. It took a lot of power to get it to roll but once it was moving it was happy to amble gently along the perimeter track with its tail gently wagging as I came to terms with the nose wheel steer.

We had been warned that a Buccaneer take-off was not going to be like the Scimitar or the Sea Vixen, but once it was cleaned up the aircraft settled down into a smooth climb. My immediate impressions were that three things, in particular, stood out. Firstly the airbrakes were very powerful and really held the aircraft back at any stage in the flight. Secondly, it was interesting to try out the selection of wheels down, and then flap down, aileron droop and tailplane flap up with the resulting production of 'blow' over the wings, flaps, ailerons and tailplane. We knew that the test pilots at Blackburns had worked very hard to find a way of making the selection of 45/25/25 easy and simple enough for the ordinary squadron pilot (ie. us) to use. In this they definitely succeeded. Thirdly, in other swept-wing jets it was possible, after landing, to pull the stick right back and use aerodynamic braking before resorting to the brakes. Once the Buccaneer was on the ground with the throttles closed, the lack of 'blow' caused the nose to rise without any encouragement from the pilot. Was it like the Firebrand? No way! Two days later it was the observers turn and after one more familiarisation trip for each of the pilots we were able to introduce them to the back seat.

In August 1961 we finally got our first two aircraft and the others followed, slowly, until we had all six of our complement. As soon as the first aircraft arrived we set about trying to put into practice the new concept of approaching the target 'under the lobe' of the enemy radar until reaching low level when the final run would be 'nap of the earth' until delivery of the weapon by long-toss attack. First of all we had to find out how far we could go in this variable height attack and this involved a lot of fuel consumption flying at various levels. The Buccaneer was very much more complex than any previous aircraft to enter the Fleet Air Arm, particularly with respect to its electronic weapons system. Unfortunately although the aircraft were 'fitted for' all this sophisticated equipment, they were not 'fitted with'. The first two or three aircraft did not have the search radar and carried a large lump of lead instead. However, once all the aircraft were properly equipped the Flight's Senior Observer, Lieutenant-Commander John Coleman was not surprised to hear one observer say 'For the first time I am carrying out all the jobs for which I was trained'. Certainly there were few idle moments in the back seat of a Buccaneer which was fully equipped with Doppler navigation radar, a roller map, TACAN, active and passive search radar plus HF and UHF communications.

It was not to be expected that introducing into service such a complicated aircraft, with a complex role, would be a easy task, but just to keep us on our toes we were also expected to introduce a new maintenance system. The normal system of carrying out Mainchecks 1, 2, 3, and 4 tended to keep aircraft out of the flying programme as the contents of the Mainchecks increased at each step. The new system broke up the sequence of checks into small packages which could be carried out while the aircraft remained available to fly. At least that was the theory but it did not take into account the many hours of engine running that was required to keep the Gyron Junior engine ready to fly. Additionally another new concept was introduced which removed the personal toolkits used by our maintainers and substituted toolkits dedicated to individual aircraft. This was backed up by the requirement that the toolkits had to be signed up as complete before the aircraft could be cleared to fly. It seemed strange at the time that people were reluctant to use the new kits instead of their tried and trusted toolkits, but I suppose tradition always was a strong point in the Navy.

As the maintainers got to know the Buccaneer better and better so the flying hours climbed and real progress was made in establishing all kinds of flight profiles. As time went by we began to get 'requests' to fly various VIPs from the south so that they could see for themselves just how good this new aircraft was. Although by this time the pilot and observer worked as a team in the operational sense, they also relied on each other when the aircraft decided to throw a 'wobbly', making sure that their response was in every way correct. A frequent problem occurred with the inlet guide vanes of the Gyron Junior engine and most crews had suffered this problem at least once and had brought the aircraft home to a safe single-engine landing. As the pilots were by now prepared to fly without their 'advisor' in the back seat, such requests were treated gracefully, if not too willingly. The flight always included a normal low level cruise through the Scottish Highlands at seven miles a minute, flipping over, almost inverted, after climbing up one side of a mountain in order to slide down the other side without popping up too high or incurring too much negative 'g'. The flight would continue by moving up to nine miles a minute for a simulated attack. After landing and after recovering they all said how much they had enjoyed the demonstration.

By June 1962 we had reached a stage where we were able to take part in a NATO exercise carrying out 'under the lobe' attacks by day and night against the Fleet. We also conducted strikes against shore targets defended by RAF Javelins and Lightnings. By the following month we were into the air display season and after taking part in displays at the RNAS bases of Yeovilton, Abbotsinch and Lossiemouth, our attention had to be drawn to taking part in the SBAC Air Display at Farnborough. At this stage in the aircraft's service no thought had been given to formation aerobatics, rather the intention was to show off the aircraft in various configurations. During practice one aircraft spun and crashed into the sea while making a steep approach to the runway. Both the crew, Lieutenant W.W. Foote USN and Lieutenant M.J. Day were killed [for details of this accident see Chapter Eleven]. Despite this mishap the Flight still had to produce a display. In order to liven up the display from a simple series of fast and slow flypasts, the leader and his number two came in fast and low over the Black Sheds and the leader rolled upside down to fly along the length of the runway, slightly behind the wingman. We heard afterwards that at least one man, Commander R.M. Crosley DSC*, the Commanding Officer of 'C' Squadron, A&AEE Boscombe Down, was impressed with this manoeuvre and was heard to say 'I never cleared a Buccaneer to do that!'

During this exciting and demanding time, I don't suppose any of us could possibly have envisaged that the Buccaneer would have such a long and distinguished career and attract such affection from so many in dark and light blue. It says a great deal about the magnetic appeal of the aircraft, based on a Staff Requirement drawn up by the Navy, and it is good that the Buccaneer Aircrew Association (BAA) continues to perpetuate its memory. Long may it do so.

No.700Z Flight carried on until 20 December 1962 when it was disbanded having flown a total of 1,258 hours on the Buccaneer S.1. The expertise that had been built up was put to good use as many of its members took up senior positions in the first operational Buccaneer units. Lieutenant-Commander Ted Anson became the commander of 801 Squadron when it was commissioned at Lossiemouth on 17 July 1962 and Alan Leahy took over at the head of 809 Squadron (also based at Lossiemouth) on 15 January 1963. The latter unit had a dual purpose as one flight carried on the work of 700Z Flight, while the other acted as a conversion outfit for new crews. As the Buccaneer had introduced a new concept in warfare, much work was undertaken in developing the weapon system and with the delivery of aircraft that were operationally fully capable, there was the opportunity to develop delivery profiles for various types of weaponry. This valuable task was carried out for the next two years and 809 Squadron was disbanded in April 1965, its role as the Royal Navy's Buccaneer conversion unit being taken on by 736 Squadron commanded by Lieutenant-Commander Willie Watson.

Buccaneer S.1
Handling Characteristics

In terms of performance the Buccaneer was a step ahead of most transonic strike aircraft of the day and its handling was rather different due to its dependence on boundary layer control to reduce landing speeds. The nearest Fleet Air Arm equivalent was the Supermarine Scimitar and many Royal Navy pilots converting onto the Buccaneer had flown this single-seat fighter/strike aircraft. Others, however, had flown the diminutive Hawker Sea Hawk which did little to prepare them for the beast from Brough. Despite the advanced nature of the Buccaneer, few had any real problems with the new aircraft, despite the fact that a dual control version of the Buccaneer was never built and most carried out successful first flights having become conversant with the relevant flight manuals. This chapter looks at some of the main points from the Handling in Flight section of Aircrew Notes for the Buccaneer S.1.

After take-off the climb out was made at a speed of 400 kts IAS converting to 0.82M as soon as that Mach number had been reached. Pilots were warned that speed was likely to increase quite slowly after take-off and the recommended technique was to use the climb up to 2,000 ft to establish the correct climbing speed. One of the idiosyncrasies of the boundary layer control installation soon made itself felt as a muffled thud was often to be heard whenever the blowing system was switched on or off due to the operation of the turbine cooling vanes. The crew was also likely to be regaled at certain times by other noises which were caused by engine-intake banging. This usually occurred at high altitude when flying in the buffet, or whenever excessive incidence was applied. It could also set in when slam accelerations were attempted. In some cases this phenomenon could be quite severe and was often accompanied by a rumbling noise from the engines and occasionally by airframe vibration. It was also possible for a flame out to be experienced on one or both engines. Although usually associated with high-altitude flight it was not unknown for intake banging to be experienced at low level, especially when pulling 'g' at relatively low airspeeds. In all cases it could be eliminated by reducing incidence and/or engine rpm.

The flying controls of the Buccaneer were fully powered, the ailerons having spring feel incorporated to provide increasing force with stick displacement. Some adverse aileron yaw was likely to be experienced when aileron was applied and this was more marked when the ailerons were drooped in the landing configuration. Throughout much of the speed range aileron forces were light with good response, however, there was some deterioration at speeds above 0.9M and when droop was applied. Response in the latter case could be improved by selecting low-speed aileron gearing, but pilots were warned that this was not to be used above 250 knots as the rates of roll that could be achieved with this gearing could easily exceed the aircraft's structural limitations.

As far as the tailplane was concerned a Q-feel system applied increased force to control column movements as speed was increased. It was recommended that autostabilisation be used below 0.9M to avoid over-controlling as the response to fore-and-aft stick was sensitive. A Q-feel system was also fitted to the rudder controls to ensure that response to rudder force remained constant throughout the speed range. Rudder response was described as being adequate for all normal manoeuvres. During asymmetric flight, when one engine was shut down, rudder forces were assessed as being moderate, becoming heavy at low airspeeds.

The airbrakes on the Buccaneer were extremely powerful and took around six seconds to extend to the fully open position. A slight buffet was noticeable at high speed and buffet was also caused by the jet efflux whenever the airbrakes were more than half way open. At low airspeeds this tended to mask the onset of airframe buffet. In the approach configuration airbrake buffet was quite marked above datum speed, however, there was a noticeable reduction as the datum speed was reached.

The use of autostabilisation was a must on the Buccaneer as without it the aircraft's Dutch rolling tendency, first noted during the preview at Boscombe Down, would return with a vengeance. This was particularly the case at high altitude and although damping was improved at low altitude, autostabilisation was still essential if accurate control was to be achieved, especially in turbulent conditions during a landing approach. Autostabilisation also allowed accurate height keeping to be made at low level and was beneficial as well in terms of yaw (the Buccaneer was also fitted with a separate yaw damper as a standby). Any failure of pitch autostabilisation at low level was potentially serious as a nose-down change of trim was likely to occur. Although this could easily be corrected by moving the control column backwards, it could still result in a dangerous loss of height. It was also possible for the aircraft to develop a pilot induced oscillation (PIO) in which case the recommended action was to move the stick firmly back to set up a condition of steady positive 'g'. The aircraft was also subject to various lateral and directional trim changes due to changes in flight conditions (undercarriage up/down etc). Most involved only a very slight change, either nose-up or nose-down, the most significant change being when the blow was switched off. This resulted in a nose-up trim change which was marked at low airspeeds.

Deliberate stalling on the Buccaneer was prohibited and pilots were requested to be aware of the warning signs that the aircraft was getting dangerously close to a stall, i.e the onset of buffet and engine-intake banging. Spinning was also to be avoided, although Aircrew Notes did include the recommended recovery technique should a pilot be foolish enough to put his aircraft in a spin. Once the direction of the spin had been ascertained, full opposite rudder had to be applied and, with the ailerons central, the control column then had to be moved progressively forwards. It was recommended that this forward movement be no more than half the available travel as excessive use of the stick was liable to result in an inverted spin. Model tests had shown that the spinning characteristics of the Buccaneer comprised an oscillation in pitch, together with a slow but varying rate of rotation with periodic hesitations. It was easy to mistake these hesitations for a recovery so it was best to maintain full anti-spin controls until it was certain that the rotation had ceased. As the aircraft stopped spinning the rudder had to be centralised and airspeed allowed to increase to 250 knots before easing out of the ensuing dive. If the correct recovery action had not been effective by the time that 15,000 ft had been reached, the crew were to abandon the aircraft (the only recorded instance of a Buccaneer being successfully recovered from a spin was by test pilot Paul Millett in XK527 during inertia coupling trials).

Despite its size, aerobatics were possible with the Buccaneer, although pilots had to be wary of inertia coupling during rolls. Vertical manoeuvres were particularly important for the Buccaneer as the standard LABS weapons delivery involved a pull up into a half loop followed by a rolling pull out. For a simulated LABS manoeuvre at a maximum all-up weight of 42,000 lb the entry height was 1,500 ft at a speed of 550 knots. With full power selected a pull up was made to 4.5 – 4.75g, the speed gradually falling to around 250-270 knots over the top. The loop was then continued until the aircraft was descending at 45 degrees and with the slip indicator central (airspeed above 350 knots) a roll out was made. If the latter manoeuvre was made at a lower airspeed there was the distinct possibility of the aircraft being subject to considerable sideslip.

During rolling manoeuvres pilots were warned that when using full stick deflection the rate of roll started gently but then increased rapidly. If a roll of more than 360 degrees was to be carried out the rate of roll would continue to increase until the aircraft became subjected to inertia coupling. This was an extremely dangerous combination of roll and yaw which could lead to loss of control and possible structural break up. The Buccaneer's powerful rudder had to be treated with caution, especially as the application of aileron during a roll produced some adverse yaw. It was important not to use the rudder coarsely in an attempt to control the yaw, or to keep the nose up when the wings were vertical. Control inputs in yaw and pitch had to be watched especially when large amounts of bank had been applied as it was easy to achieve excessive angles of sideslip, negative-g or a combination of the two. This could lead to unpredictable manoeuvres with the risk of structural damage to the aircraft. This was especially so at speeds above 500 knots as adverse yaw was particularly marked and the rudder was extremely powerful.

Providing no external stores were being carried, full stick deflection could be used to perform a roll of up to 360 degrees between 300 kts IAS and 0.85M in 1g flight, however, for such a manoeuvre the autostabilisers had to be on and the aileron gear change had to be at the high speed setting. During a roll it was also recommended that the stick should not be moved in the fore-and-aft direction and that any height corrections should be made when the wings were in the level position on completion of the roll. If external stores were being carried, the second half of a 360 degree roll had to be completed very carefully with reduced use of aileron. At speeds below 300 kts IAS and above 0.85M there were rather more restrictions as full lateral stick deflection could only be used in 1g flight to reverse a turn by rolling through the upright position. A significant pause had to be made before reversing the roll and the aileron was not to be applied rapidly. The roll also had to be stopped with less than 90 degrees of bank applied.

In flight conditions of less than 1g the ailerons had to be used very gently and the application of full stick deflection was to be avoided. Rolls also had to be restricted to 90 degrees of bank, except that a roll off the top was acceptable. Simultaneous coarse application of tailplane and aileron was to be avoided as this was likely to induce severe inertia coupling which was liable to lead to loss of control. When the Buccaneer was being designed the phenomenon of inertia coupling was new and was brought about by the trend towards longer and heavier fuselages and relatively small aerodynamic surfaces. This significantly altered the fore-and-aft mass distribution and the dumb-bell effect created was liable to set up a motion that the wings and tail could not control. Excessive manoeuvring along one axis was also likely to lead to a couple developing, for example large angles of roll could well lead to pitch and the forces were such that structural break up was a distinct possibility. To avoid inertia coupling with the Buccaneer it was recommended that the controls be used gently and that at no time should a loading of 4g be exceeded. When carrying anything other than empty drop tanks, the bank angle limit was 60 degrees and during rolling pull outs, a loading of 3g had not to be exceeded. In the normal circuit configuration, full aileron could be used to execute normal circuit manoeuvres. Deliberate and sustained inverted flight was prohibited and any flight carried out in conditions of less than 1g was limited to a maximum period of ten seconds.

As recounted above, inertia coupling was a particular hazard for Buccaneer crews and could be induced by coarse application of aileron during the initial stages of a rolling manoeuvre or by exceeding the maximum permissible angle of roll, particularly when the aircraft was subject to less than 1g. If either of these conditions occurred the aircraft's inertia tended to override the effect of the controls and was liable to generate violent gyrations in yaw and pitch. These would occur without warning and result in sudden loss of control. If the aircraft was being flown at high IAS at the time it was probable that structural damage would be the result. In such circumstances the best that the pilot could do was to centralise the controls which was best done by merely releasing the controls. The temptation to use the tailplane and rudder controls in an attempt to control pitch and yaw had to be resisted as this was likely to aggravate the situation and bring about a stall or a spin.

Above 30,000 ft the maximum Mach number obtainable in level flight at full power varied with height but generally was in the range 0.89 – 0.92M. The limiting Mach number of the Buccaneer was 0.95M and this could be achieved in a gentle dive. Between 0.88M and 0.91M there was some slight intermittent buffet, but above these speeds flight became smooth again. Any accelerations applied during turns or during the recovery from dives was likely to induce airframe buffet or engine-intake banging. The latter could be severe on occasions and in extreme cases could lead to flame out. At low level (2,000 ft and below) the limiting airspeed was 580 knots and this could be achieved on less than full power. At this speed the aircraft was generally pleasant to fly with an excellent view. It also had ease of control and good manoeuvrability. At a speed of 580 knots an acceleration of 6g could be applied without inducing buffet.

Air-to-air refuelling with the Buccaneer S.1 was permitted with Scimitar and Sea Vixen tankers equipped with Mk.20A pods and collapsible drogues and could be carried out at any altitude between 2,000 ft and 35,000 ft. The minimum and maximum speeds for refuelling operations were 230 knots and 290 knots. Normally air-to-air refuelling was relatively easy to accomplish, although it tended to become more difficult at altitudes above 20,000 ft. When making a contact at 20,000 ft or below the recommended speed was 250 knots. When the tanker was ready to accept the receiver, pilots were requested to close on the tanker in a slight climb with an overtake speed of 2-3 knots. When closing in the best technique was to focus on the tanker aircraft and not to become too fixated with the drogue which would probably be bobbing around slightly in the slipstream. In most cases last minute corrections to the flight path would not be necessary.

Refuelling became progressively more difficult at altitudes above 20,000 ft and there was an increased risk of the drogue coming into contact with the radome and causing damage. It was recommended that the roll and yaw channels of the autostabiliser be switched to the approach setting as control would be easier. In the event of a missed contact, the aircraft was to be eased back by gentle throttle movement to a position about five yards behind the drogue before making a further approach. When in contact with the drogue, normal formation flying techniques were to be applied. With a Sea Vixen tanker it was acceptable to fly at the normal trailing position of the hose but in the case of the Scimitar it was more comfortable to fly about four feet below this position in order to ensure that the Buccaneer's T-tail was out of the tanker's jet wake. When refuelling was complete a withdrawal was made by reducing power. Having broken contact it was best to fly away slightly below the trailing line of the hose as there was a danger, especially in conditions of turbulence, that the drogue might hit the radome.

The Buccaneer S.1 was originally designed with a retractable refuelling probe, however, this proved to be a complete failure as in the extended position it was rather too close to the nose section, the bow wave from which affected the aerodynamics of the drogue so that making a successful contact was extremely difficult. If the pilot did manage to hook up to the drogue his problems were far from over as airflow disturbance from the probe/drogue combination was likely to lead to a compressor stall in the engine. Although early examples of the Buccaneer S.1 did feature a retractable refuelling probe the whole concept had to be abandoned and on subsequent aircraft a fixed probe was used instead.

The saga recounted above led to an amusing incident at Lossiemouth. An RAF navigator on an exchange posting with the Fleet Air Arm recalls a flight he made during his conversion course with 736 Squadron. This would normally have been carried out on a Buccaneer S.2 (the remaining examples of the S.1 being flown by the newly formed RAF OCU course) but due to aircraft unserviceability it was necessary to carry out a sortie in an old S.1. During the flight his pilot was troubled by a green-coloured button in the cockpit, especially as he had no idea what it was for. Eventually curiosity got the better of him and reasoning that as the button was painted green, and therefore could not be too dangerous, decided to give it a press. The crew then got the shock of their lives as a retractable refuelling probe lumbered into view, the noise of this process being akin to that of a car crashing.

When descending from altitude the airbrakes proved to be very effective and allowed steep descents to be made without incurring excessively high airspeeds. Normal descents were made at 85 per cent rpm, airbrakes out, at 300 kts IAS. This resulted in a descent of approximately 12,000 ft/min. When it was necessary to carry out a maximum rate descent, rpm was reduced to a minimum of 60 per cent and with full airbrakes, the descent was flown at 0.85M or 400 kts IAS. In conditions of severe turbulence the recommended speed for crew comfort was 400 kts IAS. The Buccaneer was fitted with a windscreen wiper and a rain clearance air jet for flight in rain, however, the wiper was not to be used at airspeeds above 350 kts IAS. In conditions of heavy rain, neither system was fully effective.

When approaching to land the most important instrument as far as the pilot was concerned was the Airstream Direction Detector (ADD). This provided visual and audio information to ensure that the approach was flown at the correct speed and angle of incidence. The datum speed for an all-up weight of 30,000 lb was 123 knots and this speed was to be varied by 2 knots per 1,000 lb above or below this weight. The audio signal comprised high, medium and low tones, the high and low tones being interrupted at varying intervals to give an indication of the speed. For example, the high tone was interrupted ten times per second at 143 knots, but only once per second at 124.5 knots. The datum speed of 123 knots (at 30,000 lb AUW) was represented by a steady medium tone.

It was important that the ADD system be calibrated accurately and this was carried out at an altitude of 2,500 ft. The aircraft was set up in the normal landing configuration (45/25/25), undercarriage down, full airbrake and with blow on. Power was maintained at 87 per cent rpm and for accurate results air conditions had to be smooth and no 'g' had to be applied. Having levelled at 2,500 ft, speed was allowed to fall to the datum for the aircraft's weight. When this speed was achieved it had to be held precisely by allowing the aircraft to descend. With datum speed being maintained in the descent, the incidence reading was noted together with the audio tone. If the ADD was correctly set up the incidence reading should have read 20 units and the audio tone should have been steady. The test was to be completed by the time that 1,500 ft had been reached. If the above readings had not been obtained, the ADD could not be relied upon as a stall warning device and was in need of ground adjustment.

The Buccaneer S.1 was cleared for single-engine flying provided that it was carried out at a height of 2,000 ft or above. An engine failure could be simulated by throttling one engine to idling rpm and then extending the airbrake to 15 degrees. When flying on one engine the single remaining flying control hydraulics system fulfilled all normal demands but the power of the Powered Flying Control Units (PFCU) was reduced and response to a sudden demand was likely to be slower. The maximum permissible speed for flight using a single flying control system was 550 kts IAS or 0.93M.

When flying with one engine shut down various services were no longer available. With the port engine stopped the roll autostabiliser facility on the port aileron, pitch and yaw stabilisation and the autopilot facility on the port aileron were all lost (the standby yaw damper was still available). In the case of the starboard engine being shut down the roll and autopilot facilities for the starboard aileron were lost, as was the standby yaw damper and Q-feel (spring feel was retained for the tailplane and rudder).

Although the engines of the Buccaneer were mounted on each side of the fuselage (unlike Armstrong Whitworth's contender for Specification M.148T which had them at mid span) there was still quite a strong asymmetric effect when flying on one engine. With the port engine stopped, the standby yaw damper had to be switched on to guard against the Buccaneer's tendency to Dutch rolling without any means of autostabilisation. The foot loads experienced by the pilot depended on speed and configuration but they were never more than about 90 lb when using full rudder at circuit speeds. Foot loads could be reduced by accurate trimming but it was impossible to trim them out completely when in the circuit and prior to landing. Approximately 25 per cent of rudder movement was required to maintain asymmetric flight at low airspeeds and this could become quite tiring if flight on one engine was prolonged.

The recommended technique for a single-engine circuit and landing was to fly the downwind leg at 1,000 ft AGL in the normal way with a flap configuration of 30/10/10, blow on and maintaining at least 91 per cent on the good engine. After lowering the undercarriage, the speed was adjusted by use of the airbrakes and the aim was to turn crosswind at 10 knots above the datum speed. This was followed by a gentle turn on to a long, straight, final approach. Engine rpm had to be maintained at 91 per cent as this was sufficient to produce the minimum permissible blow pressure of 20 PSI. When on the mirror glidepath the usual position for the airbrake was in the half open position, however, minor adjustments were to be made to maintain the correct datum speed. A normal power on landing was to be made, however, the pilot was warned not to apply the brakes when the aircraft was travelling at more than 120 knots.

Should an overshoot be necessary, the single-engine performance of the Buccaneer S.1 was critically dependent on its all-up weight. A successful overshoot could be carried out on one engine assuming that the flap configuration was 30/10/10 and that the aircraft was at the datum speed with blow on. The airbrakes also had to be fully in and the undercarriage had to be retracted. Due to this requirement the decision to overshoot had to be made by 200 ft as this allowed a period of time for the airbrakes to close and the undercarriage to retract. Provided that the all-up weight of the aircraft was less than 31,000 lb, it was possible to carry out a touch-and-go under ISA conditions. The maintaining of datum speed, both during the approach and on the overshoot, was critical. If speed was allowed to fall below the correct datum figure then the subsequent climb performance would be severely affected. To carry out an overshoot the recommended technique was to open the throttle fully on the live engine, close the airbrakes, raise the undercarriage and climb initially at the datum speed. If it was possible for the speed to be increased by 10 knots an improved rate of climb would result.

When considering a single-engine deck landing the maximum all-up weight was 30,600 lb and the 30/10/10 configuration had to be adopted. If the fuel state permitted it was best to carry out a slow speed handling check and overshoot practice at a safe height (around 2,000 ft) before attempting a landing. In order to ensure that adequate blow pressure was maintained, power had to remain in the region of 90 per cent rpm. Any reduction in airspeed that was required was achieved by careful use of the airbrakes rather than by a large reduction in engine rpm which was liable to cause fluctuations in the blow pressure. During the final stages of the approach the airbrakes needed to be extended by more than half of their available extension. At touchdown full power was to be selected on the good engine whilst simultaneously selecting airbrakes in. Under ISA conditions, at the maximum AUW of 30,600 lb, an overshoot was possible at any stage of the approach. With half extension of the airbrakes and with undercarriage down, the aircraft would climb at around 138-140 kts IAS. In the event of a 'bolter' occurring, the airbrakes had to be selected in and the undercarriage retracted as soon as possible.

To relight an engine the correct procedure was to check that the engine master cock was on and that the blow was off (except in an emergency). The relight button was then pressed and the throttle opened to the ground idle position. Light up was indicated by an increase in the Jet Pipe Temperature (JPT) gauge, together with idling rpm. A pause of ten seconds then had to be allowed with the throttle at the idling position. The generator was also switched on and light up could be accompanied by a slight thump. If no relight was achieved after 30 seconds, the relight button had to be released and the HP cock closed. There was then a one minute wait to allow excess fuel to drain before another attempt could be made. If a relight had been unsuccessful it was recommended that a second attempt be made at a lower altitude. During the relight it was important that JPT should not rise above 600 degrees C.

When an aircraft was being flown with one engine throttled at a low airspeed, and in the circuit configuration with blow on, it was highly likely that the idling engine would fail to accelerate when the throttle was opened. In this case the rpm would remain at idling and there was every chance that there would be a rapid rise in JPT. If this occurred the throttle had to be closed and a further attempt made when the aircraft had been cleaned up and the blow was off. On completion of practice single-engine flying the minimum altitude was 2,000 ft and the aircraft could only descend below this altitude when the idling engine had been accelerated back to normal operation.

First Impressions

T he Buccaneer was an imposing aircraft, especially on first acquaintance, and pilots who were confronted with it during their conversion course could be forgiven for feeling a certain amount of trepidation at the prospect of having to take it into the air. As no twin-stick Buccaneer was ever produced, any nerves in the front cockpit were likely to be matched by the instructor sitting in the navigator's position directly behind! The following accounts offer an insight into pilots' first impressions of the Buccaneer, its handling characteristics and comparisons with some of its contemporaries.

Group Captain Tom Eeles had a long association with the Buccaneer and first flew the aircraft with 801 Squadron during an exchange posting with the Fleet Air Arm. He then went on to become a QFI with 736 Squadron, the Navy conversion unit for the Buccaneer. His experience of the Buccaneer in RAF service comprised no less than three tours with 237 OCU, the last as the unit's CO, and a tour with 12 Squadron. He was also awarded the Queen's Commendation for Valuable Service in the Air.

The first thing you noticed as you walked out to a Buccaneer was its size – it was a big beast, weighing in at around 20 tons, 64 feet long and with a wingspan of 44 feet. It was quite a climb up into the cockpit, which was fitted with Martin Baker Mk.6 MSB ejection seats. Early Naval aircraft had an underwater ejection system fitted to the seat, this was replaced later by a rocket pack, giving a 'zero/zero' capability. Cockpit instrumentation was somewhat haphazard. The excellent OR946 Integrated Flight Instrument System, driven by a Master Reference Gyro and an Air Data Computer, was rather overshadowed by the proliferation of other random instruments; these seemed to increase every time a modification was embodied. By the end of the aircraft's life the cockpit could best be described as an ergonomic slum.

In front of the pilot was the Strike Sight, a simple head-up display which used a sight glass that could be folded down to improve forward visibility. The aircraft also had a very effective windscreen clearance hot air jet and a wiper/washer (just like your car), both essential for operations over the sea. The twin Speys, or Gyron Juniors in the S.1, were started by using an external low-pressure air starter, there being no on-board starter system, something to be borne in mind when operating away from home base. Once the engines were running and the various systems had been checked, taxiing was straightforward, there being ample power and authority from the brakes and nose wheel steering.

Catapult launch from a carrier was 'hands off'; tailplane angle was set so that the aircraft would rotate a small amount on leaving the deck, mainplane flap/aileron droop/tailplane flap was set to its maximum deflection of 45/25/25 with the Boundary Layer Control (BLC) system on, the aircraft was tensioned up on the catapult in the launch attitude and full power applied. When ready to launch the pilot would brace his left arm to ensure full power remained applied, raise his right hand to indicate he was ready to go to the Flight Deck Officer, then place it on his right thigh adjacent to, but not holding the control column. Acceleration down the catapult was very brisk and once airborne the pilot would take control whilst being careful not to induce a high pitch rate, as the Buccaneer was unstable in pitch at low speed. After retracting the landing gear and cleaning up the flap and droop in stages, the aircraft accelerated quickly to its normal operating speed of 420-480 knots. Take-offs from runways were carried out unblown with flap/droop set to 15/10/10, unless aircraft weight or runway length required a blown take-off, when flap/droop was set to 30/20/20.

Both Marks of Buccaneer were a delight to handle when in their element of high speed at low level, however, the S.1 was rather underpowered. Control forces were well balanced and light. The maximum permitted speed was 580 knots or 0.95M, which could be maintained for ages and easily exceeded. Because of the need to fit the Buccaneer into aircraft carrier hangar decks, the fin was relatively short so at high speed the aircraft was a bit unstable in yaw. Aileron rolls, barrel rolls and rolls off the top of loops were permitted but full loops were not. The aircraft could suffer from inertia coupling if certain handling limitations were ignored. Toss attack profiles were initiated at 540 knots, dive and level attack profiles were flown in the 450-500 knot range. The very wide range of weapons available made for challenging and exciting flying; the Buccaneer was an excellent weapons platform.

When speed was reduced below 300 knots for recovery the Buccaneer became much more difficult to fly accurately. Approaches were normally flown in the 45/25/25 BLC on configuration, airbrake fully extended, with the final approach being flown at a constant speed for a no flare landing. The excellent Airstream Direction Detector (ADD) gave both audio and visual indication of angle of attack/airspeed allowing the pilot to keep his eyesight out of the cockpit – essential for accurate deck landings. The basic final approach speed (blown) was 127 knots, considerably lower than similar fast jets. It increased to 155 knots unblown. Single engine approaches could be flown either blown at 30/20/20 (essential if landing on a carrier) or unblown at 45/10/10, the usual option for an airfield landing. There was no asymmetric handling problem and the S.2 could overshoot on one engine from the threshold providing that the fuel state was well down. Arrested landings, both afloat and ashore, were straightforward. After 8,000 hours of military flying on many different types I still feel that my 2,185 hours on the Buccaneer, both at sea and shore based, were the most demanding and exciting of my flying career.

Don Headley first flew a Buccaneer on 18 January 1966 as part of his work as a ferry pilot. Having flown Vampire, Venom and Javelin aircraft in the RAF, Don joined the Navy ferry unit which was run by the Air Services Division of Short Brothers and was based at Rochester, moving to West Malling when this airfield was vacated by the RAF. His first flight in a Buccaneer was not exactly straightforward as he recalls,

When I was ferrying for the Navy I was mainly flying Sea Vixens and Hunters. One day my boss mentioned that he wanted me to convert to the Buccaneer as only one other pilot on the Ferry Flight was qualified to fly it. I was to go up to Lossiemouth to train on the simulator but unfortunately when I got there it had gone unserviceable and remained so whilst I was there. My next job was to go to Holme-on-Spalding Moor to convert onto the aeroplane properly with the flight test team at Hawker Siddeley. They gave me a new Buccaneer S.2 (XT287) that had just come off its production test schedule and designated Mike Addley as my flight test observer. We had a full briefing from the systems people and taxied to the end of the runway with Mike reading the check lists from the back. The take-off was 15-10-10 unblown and during the climb out I tried the ailerons. As speed built up to 400 knots I remember saying 'This is fantastic, there is a lovely feel on this aeroplane' when there was a loud bang and the aeroplane rolled rapidly. I knew immediately what had happened as I had forgotten to pull the flaps in.

I thought initially that a flap had broken off and so I called the

Tower and told them about our problem. They advised us to burn off fuel and then come in for a flapless landing. So it was that I came in for my very first landing in a Buccaneer and as it was flapless, it was very fast at around 146 knots. I can guarantee to this day that I landed on the piano keys on the 2,000 yard runway at exactly the speed they had given me. Afterwards I apologised profusely for breaking a brand new aeroplane and felt very sorry for myself. They just said 'It's all right, we'll fix it, the Navy will pay!' It transpired that the flap had not actually broken off but a torque tube had sheared. I then had another flight in a Buccaneer and on my third trip I was asked if I would take it to Lossiemouth to deliver it. Some time later, after I had joined Hawker Siddeley, I found that J.G. 'Bobby' Burns, a test pilot, had also broken a flap and it wasn't that uncommon.

Thereafter each subsequent flight was just like a first solo as we only went to pick up new aeroplanes and so I could easily go for a month or two without flying a Buccaneer. On delivery flights there was no one in the back seat as we could not afford a navigator or observer. I used to fly to Lossiemouth offering a silent prayer 'Please God, let nothing go wrong!' One thing did, however, exacerbate matters. There had been a spate of what were thought to be runaway tailplane trims. To get round this problem, if it happened, the observers had been briefed to pull out the fuse in the trim circuit, but when the aeroplane was being flown solo, as was the case on delivery flights, a piece of string was fastened to the fuse and then routed along the left-hand wall of the cockpit into the pilot's cabin so that it could be pulled if necessary. Unfortunately this just meant that there was a much greater risk of doing yourself out of tailplane trim as it was far too easy to catch the string inadvertently and pull the fuse out. In the end it was discovered that it was not runaway tailplane trim at all, it turned out that the trim button adjacent to the pilot's thumb was just too easy to pull back when the aeroplane went into a pull-up for a toss manoeuvre. There is one certain naval gentleman who has been known as 'Thumbs' ever since!

The Buccaneer was the most advanced aeroplane that I had flown up to that time. With blown leading and trailing edges, blown ailerons and tailplane and rotating bomb-doors it was a very complicated aeroplane. From the pilot's point of view complications also resulted due to the fact that to maintain the necessary blow, you had to keep power on the engines. This meant that big airbrakes were necessary to give the drag required to overcome the unwanted thrust. It was a remarkable aeroplane to combine its weight, performance and carrying capacity, and still be capable of fitting into British aircraft carriers. This was why it folded at the front and back, as well as the wings.

When you first got into a Buccaneer after, say, a single-seat Hunter, the cockpit felt huge, but later when I was flying both the Phantom and Buccaneer from Holme-on-Spalding Moor it felt quite small after the F-4. The trouble with the Buccaneer cockpit was that so much instrumentation was scattered around in it. The back cockpit was the worst and when you looked in there it really was dreadful the way things had been chucked in almost as an afterthought. I did not like the throttles on the Buccaneer as these came back to a sideways cut-off which acted like a High Pressure fuel cock on other aeroplanes. You pulled the throttles back, moved them to one side and back again to shut the engines down. However, with use the shoulders could round off on the stop and it was only too easy inadvertently to pull the throttles all the way back. This was a particular concern during a crosswind landing when you were kicking rudder on and pulling the throttles back quickly. On one occasion it happened to me and the throttles came right back through the stops and I ended up with two engines out, although I managed to relight one still on the runway.

The lookout from the Buccaneer cockpit was not too bad but due to the thick windscreen and its associated pillars it was not as good as you would expect from a fighter-type aeroplane. During briefing you had to tell people to keep moving their heads to avoid blindspots. The view to the rear was a bit restricted but this was aided by a large rear view mirror.

The Buccaneer had a very high wing loading and rates as the nicest aeroplane I have ever flown at low level in rough conditions; it was like sitting in an armchair at home at 100 ft over the sea at 580 knots and was very comfortable indeed. Above 25,000 ft, however, it was a completely different matter. When you tried to turn it was a bit of a pig as it did not have the wing area to do it. One item that I did not like on the Buccaneer was the autopilot which I never really trusted at high speed and low level and I felt that this could have been improved greatly.

Group Captain Mike Shaw came to the Buccaneer relatively late in his RAF career when he took over as Station Commander at RAF Honington in 1980. His first familiarisation flight was in XT281 on 13 November 1979 with Tom Eeles accompanying him in the rear seat. With nearly 1,400 hours on the F-4 Phantom, Mike was finally able to appreciate an aircraft that he had previously seen mostly through a gunsight,

Having spent eighteen years in air defence, it certainly came as something of a surprise when I was posted to RAF Honington as Station Commander. I had never really come across the Buccaneer all that much except when trying to shoot it down, but I knew that it could be a real swine to get, especially when coming in over the North Sea at low level. The Phantom had a pulse Doppler radar which would pick out relative movement and as long as a target was heading towards you at more than 70 knots you would see it as a blip. When a lock-on had been achieved you would discover the target range but until then the only information available was azimuth and closing speed. In those days anything coming at you at high speed at low level was either an F-111 or a Buccaneer – both were difficult targets but the Buccaneer was more agile and once it knew that you had locked it up it would throw a turn, left or right, and once it was down to zero Doppler shift, which meant that it was not closing on you anymore (except with your own closing speed), it would just disappear from the screen. Then, of course, you could not shoot because the Sparrow missile would not guide.

Assuming that you made the right decision as to which way the Buccaneer had turned you would descend to low level to try and chase it but it would invariably be doing 520 knots or more. In a Phantom at low level that was beginning to get a bit tricky because when you trimmed at high speed, the control column moved away from you. On the Buccaneer when you trimmed, the tailplane moved but the stick did not, so whatever speed you were doing in a Buccaneer, the stick was always comfortable in the neutral position. At high speed and low level the Phantom was physically very tiring to fly as the stick was so far forward that you were reaching for it. With the Buccaneer it was in the same place all the time, just by your knees, which was the perfect position. I always felt that if a Buccaneer pilot knew what he was doing, he stood a good chance of getting away. The Buccaneer was also cleared down to 100 ft and the Phantom was not very happy down there at all; 250ft was as low as we would ever want to go in training. If we had ever got into a position to fire a Sidewinder missile at 100 ft it would probably have fused on the wave tops! The Buccaneer would often get away simply because it flew so low and so fast.

I always found the Buccaneer to be a challenge and when I got the chance to fly it I could see why it had been such a difficult opponent. I flew it down to 100 ft or so over the sea and at that height you had to watch out for oil rigs and ships. You had to be very wary and could not relax for a moment but the aircraft itself felt very solid and rode the bumps pretty well. At speeds below 300 knots the handling was not as good and it was not as pleasant to fly, requiring quite a bit of rudder to balance a turn. Once the gear and flaps were down, however, it improved again and it was very stable at speeds of 150 knots or less. With BLC on, you were fooling the wings by blowing hot air over them and they thought they were going 20 knots faster than they were. BLC was what kept you in the air when you were going slowly but the Buccaneer was quite nice to handle in that configuration. Although the Gyron Junior engines of the S.1 were rather underpowered, I found that the Spey engines on the S.2 were exactly right for the job that the Buccaneer had to do; any more power would have been of no use whatsoever, and I never had a moment's worry about the engines.

The cockpit of the Buccaneer was quite small and there was not much room for the navigator with his instruments and his radar behind the pilot's ejection seat. The navigator was quite close to you and was always looking over your right shoulder as he sat slightly higher and his seat was offset a few inches to the right. He could see various instruments in the front cockpit such as the blow gauges and the engine rpm gauges and could thus monitor a bit of what the pilot was doing. He also had some forward view. For me it was a strange feeling at first to have someone peering over my shoulder all the time as on the Phantom the navigator sat further back, and although he was positioned a little higher he had no forward view at all.

The undercarriage on the Buccaneer was a wonderful piece of design which would come up in 2 seconds after you pressed the button to retract it. I have never known an undercarriage retract like that, especially as it was big and extremely heavy. I did, however, have one minor complaint and that was the nosewheel steering which because of the caster angle on the nosewheel leg was not very positive. The button that operated it was on the inboard throttle and you really needed a double-jointed wrist to get your thumb on the button. The Phantom just had a button on the stick and the knuckle on your right thumb would rest on it. All arrivals in the Buccaneer were carrier-type, no flare landings, you just crashed it into the ground and the undercarriage soaked it up.

As regards top speed you could hold the Buccaneer at the limiting speed of 580 kts IAS with something less than full power so there was a bit left. When you were doing this kind of speed it was so noisy that you could not talk with your navigator in the back. It was certainly not a pleasant experience and we only went to 580 knots on the odd occasion. I did, however, see 520-540 kts IAS quite often, which was not something I was used to as in the Phantom we tended to cruise at around 420 kts IAS.

During my time at Honington I also flew the Tornado GR.1 which was just coming into service. Compared with the Buccaneer it was quiet. One reason for this was that the microphones in both cockpits did not become live until you spoke, when it acted like any other microphone by picking up all the cockpit noise. When neither pilot nor navigator was speaking the cockpit was very quiet, even when the IAS was above 500 knots. The ride in the Buccaneer was good although I found it to be a little bumpier than the Tornado as it did not have the advanced systems for taking out the bumps electronically. One thing I did not like on the Tornado was the fact that it had to carry all its bombs externally, which created a lot of drag and the need for extra power to overcome it. On the Buccaneer, of course, there was a large internal bomb bay, the door of which was modified to house an extra 3,000 lb of fuel. Although the Tornado was a fine aeroplane, it could not go as far as a Buccaneer (without air-to-air refuelling) and it could not go as fast at low level. When the GR.1 first arrived at Honington we all said that what 'they' should have done was to put the Tornado radar, which was extremely good, and all the systems into the Buccaneer. If they had done that we would have had a really excellent low-level bomber!'

The Buccaneer S.2

Even before the S.1 had entered service, plans had already been made to replace it with a more advanced version and this resulted in the Buccaneer S.2. Although the S.1 was a capable aircraft which could perform the role for which it was intended, it did suffer from certain restrictions. One of its main drawbacks was a lack of power which meant that certain aspects of its performance were extremely marginal following the loss of an engine. It was also restricted in range which meant that for some missions it was necessary to launch the aircraft at less than all-up weight and then engage in air-to-air refuelling with Scimitar tankers before carrying out the remainder of the sortie.

The original naval requirement had been to get a suitable strike aircraft in service as quickly as possible and although the Blackburn design had been chosen as the best that would be available in a reasonable timescale, it was also recognised that it was likely to be replaced by an updated variant at an early stage in its life. The choice of engine for the new aircraft lay between a development of the Gyron Junior, an advanced Orpheus engine from Bristol Siddeley and a military version of the Spey that had been designed by Rolls-Royce for the de Havilland DH.121 airliner which was to become well known as the Hawker Siddeley Trident. At 9,000 lb thrust (8,340 lb when BLC was in operation) the Orpheus was the least powerful engine and was quickly discarded. The new Gyron Junior offered nearly 11,000 lb of thrust but it lost out as major structural alterations would have been needed to the Buccaneer airframe.

The final contender was the Rolls-Royce Spey which was rated at just over 11,000 lb thrust, sufficient to make a big difference to the Buccaneer's performance, and it could be fitted without major modification work. As it was also calculated that the range of a Spey-engined Buccaneer would be 80 per cent greater than the S.1 (more than twice that of the other contenders) the Spey was obviously the way to go. The increased range of the Buccaneer S.2 was to be graphically illustrated on 4 October 1965 when XN974 was flown non-stop across the Atlantic from Goose Bay in Labrador to Lossiemouth, thereby becoming the first Fleet Air Arm aircraft to achieve this feat (whilst in the US, XN974, together with XK527 and XN976, had undertaken tropical trials at NAS Pensacola in Florida and had also performed deck trials aboard the USS *Lexington*).

To accommodate an 80 per cent increase in mass flow, the air intakes had to be enlarged considerably and were made oval in shape instead of circular as on the S.1. The jet pipes were also of a modified design. Other significant aerodynamic changes included the installation of inner-wing leading edge boundary layer control and changes to the BLC slit sizes and locations on the outer-wing leading edge, flap shroud and tailplane leading edge. The BLC installation was simplified by a reduction in the number of control valves in the duct system. Air for the BLC system was taken from tappings on the seventh stage of the high pressure compressors. Another major difference lay in the electrical system as the 28v DC electrical system of the S.1 was replaced by two 30 kva AC generators which provided the primary source of electrical power.

The first Buccaneer to be converted as an S.2 was XK526, a development batch machine that had been involved on trials work at Holme-on-Spalding Moor since its first flight on 29 August 1960. The first flight in its new guise was on 18 April 1963 and it was soon joined by XK527 in the development programme, an on-going process which was not without its problems. The redesign of the nacelles and jet pipes to accommodate the Spey engines of the S.2 led to a significant increase in drag at cruising speeds and it was found that some re-profiling was necessary at the back end. This did manage to reduce the amount of drag that was being created, but not to the level that had been predicted. In an effort to improve cruise performance at high altitude the trailing edges of the wing tips were extended outwards. Although there was only a marginal increase in wing area, cruise performance was improved, however, this modification was to proved costly many years later as it set up structural stresses that were to be a major factor in causing fatigue problems.

The first deck landing of a Buccaneer S.2 took place in September 1964 when XN974, the first production aircraft, made eight launches and arrested landings on HMS *Eagle*. At the time this aircraft was fitted with what was known as 'dovetail' standard Spey engines, however, by March 1965, when a more extensive trial was carried out using HMS *Ark Royal*, it had been fitted with 'straight T slot' Spey engines. During the latter trial XN974 was joined by XN975 which had the most up-to-date Spey then available and was known as the 'skewed T slot'. These terms referred to different compressor standards of Spey engine, all of which, at one time or another, were fitted to Buccaneer S.2s in Royal Navy service. Apart from the variation in engine standards, both aircraft allocated for the deck trials were to a similar modification standard which included Mod.631 (underwater escape). Special instrumentation was fitted to both aircraft, and this was used throughout the trials to obtain

he first pre-production NA.39 (XK486) seen on an early test flight. (via Philip Jarrett)

nother view of XK486 showing the clam-shell airbrakes in the fully open position. (via Philip Jarrett)

NA.39 XK489 was flown for the first time on 28 January 1959 and was used for trials at HOSM and Boscombe Down. Note the difference in nose profile with the first prototypes. (via author)

XK490 in the landing configuration with gear and airbrakes extended. This aircraft was involved in fatal accident on 12 October 1959. (via Philip Jarrett)

The first deck trials with the NA.39 were carried out in January 1960. XK523 is seen shortly after launch from HMS *Victorious*. (via Philip Jarrett)

NA.39 XK491 during flight refuelling trials with Canberra B.2 WH734. (Flight Refuelling via Philip Jarrett)

Blackburn test pilot J.G. 'Bobby' Burns poses with an NA.39 in January 1961. The pod on the ground was an airborne version of the starter trolley that could be fitted to a weapons pylon when an away landing was planned. (via Philip Jarrett)

XK530 gets airborne from the steam catapult at RAE Bedford in August 1961. (RAE Bedford via Philip Jarrett)

XK489 takes a wire during arrested landing trials. (RAE Bedford via Philip Jarrett)

First flown on 18 May 1961, XK531 was the first aircraft to join 700Z Flight, the Royal Navy's Intensive Flying Trials Unit, at Lossiemouth. (via Philip Jarrett)

XK526 is seen in its element at ultra low level in May 1962. (via Philip Jarrett)

The penultimate NA.39, XK534 displays the white anti-flash colour scheme adopted in the early 1960s. This picture shows it during service with 700Z Flight. (Flight via Philip Jarrett)

Buccaneer S.1 XN965 gets airborne from the angled flight deck of HMS *Eagle* in July 1964. (Crown Copyright via Philip Jarrett)

Another view of XK526 at low level. (via Philip Jarrett)

A Buccaneer S.1 flies over HMS *Puma*, a Leopard class frigate. (Crown Copyright via Philip Jarrett)

A busy deck scene on board HMS *Hermes* in May 1962 showing a 700Z Flight Buccaneer S.1. (Crown Copyright via Philip Jarrett)

A Buccaneer S.1 about to land on HMS *Hermes* on 30 August 1961. (Crown Copyright via Philip Jarrett)

Buccaneer S.1 XN949 of 801 Squadron on the deck of HMS *Victorious*. (Crown Copyright via Philip Jarrett)

Armed with four 1,000 lb bombs on the underwing pylons, Buccaneer S.1 XN953 of 800 Squadron is seen shortly before launch from HMS *Eagle*. (via Philip Jarrett)

801 Squadron Buccaneer S.1 XN948 from HMS *Victorious* launches a Bullpup air-to-surface missile. (via Philip Jarrett)

Another view of S.1 XN948 of 801 Squadron following a landing mishap on HMS *Victorious*. (via Philip Jarrett)

HMS *Eagle* passes through the Suez Canal, its Buccaneers ranged on deck with XN959 of 800 Squadron in the foreground. (via Philip Jarrett)

Destined for the South African Air Force, this Buccaneer S.50 is pictured at Elvington during rocket-assisted take-off trials. (via Philip Jarrett)

SAAF Buccaneer S.50 armed with four Nord AS.30 air-to-surface missiles. (via Philip Jarrett)

Buccaneer S.2 XT269 of 700B Flight flies low over on HMS *Victorious*. (via Philip Jarrett)

A Buccaneer S.2 and crew with the wide range of weaponry that the aircraft was capable of carrying. Prominent in the foreground is the Red Beard nuclear bomb. (via Philip Jarrett)

Royal Navy strike aircraft old and new. Buccaneer S.2 XV156 of 800 Squadron formates on Fairey Swordfish LS326 of the Royal Navy Historic Flight. (via Philip Jarrett)

Buccaneer S.2 XV152 is pictured at RNAS Yeovilton in April 1967. (via Philip Jarrett)

A Buccaneer S.2 (XV152) over the deck of HMS *Hermes*. (via Philip Jarrett)

S.2 XN980 of 801 Squadron flies close to Waterloo Station, London. This aircraft was lost on 3 March 1969 when it collided with XV159 near Wick. (via Philip Jarrett)

quantitative data. The trial aboard HMS *Ark Royal* resulted in 78 launches and landings and the data obtained, together with that from HMS *Eagle*, enabled the issue of the Buccaneer S.2's interim CA release for carrier operations.

The weight limits for the S.2 were considerably higher than those of the S.1. Catapult launching of the S.2 was restricted to an all-up weight of 50,000 lb, a figure that was actually 3,500 lb below the aircraft's maximum all-up weight, however this lower figure had to be used to comply with carrier deck strength limitations. The deciding factor during landings was undercarriage strength and the maximum deck landing weight was 35,000 lb, or 37,000 lb under emergency conditions. Although the S.2 was different from the S.1 in many ways, in others it appeared to have changed very little. During taxiing, pilots still had difficulty with the nosewheel, particularly at the higher all-up weights, and this was criticised for its limited authority (+/-50 degrees). There was also an apparent lag in response to pilot demand. Due to these limitations, and a lag in engine response to throttle movements in the idle to 85 per cent rpm range, manoeuvring on deck was imprecise and necessitated the coarse use of brakes and throttle.

As a result of experience with the Buccaneer S.1 during catapult launches, a revised technique was eventually adopted whereby the tailplane trim was set prior to launch and during the launch itself the pilot did not touch the control column, only taking hold of it when airborne. This was to avoid any tendency towards high angles of incidence after take off caused by the pilot making inadvertent fore-and-aft control column movements during the launching run which could lead to excessive pitch-up. The primary aim of the trials in HMS *Eagle* was to assess this so-called 'in trim' catapult launching technique for the S.2 which had its CG position further forward than the S.1 due to changes to the BLC installation and jet pipe geometry. The revised CG meant that it was necessary to set more negative tailplane trim on the S.2 (the setting depended on aircraft loading and launching speed but was approximately -7 degrees on the S.2 as compared with -4 degrees with the S.1).

The trials in HMS *Eagle* confirmed the suitability of the 'in trim' technique for the Buccaneer S.2 and the more comprehensive trials aboard HMS *Ark Royal* showed that it was satisfactory for all loadings, except the condition where the external fuel tanks were empty. Due to a reduction in longitudinal stability when the tanks were empty of fuel a tailplane trim setting of -5½ degrees was found to be more suitable. As on the Buccaneer S.1, flaps, aileron droop and negative tailplane flap settings were used for carrier launch and landing, the configuration adopted being 45/25/25. Minimum launch speeds recommended for initial CA release in ISA conditions were 115 kts TAS up to 42,000 lb AUW and then a linear progression up to 131 kts TAS at 50,000 lb AUW. At these speeds no significant sink was experienced and wing incidence after launch rarely exceeded 15 degrees. For service use a limiting incidence of 15 degrees was considered to give an adequate safety margin over pre-stall effects which consisted of wing drop at 18$^1/_2$ degrees of wing incidence. Acceleration after leaving the catapult was well above minimum requirements in the ambient conditions experienced during the trials.

For a normal landing with BLC on the configuration adopted was again 45/25/25. Approach speeds had already been measured during shore based trials at 127 kts IAS at 33,000 lb AUW, with a +/-2 knots correction for each 1,000 lb above or below this weight. Three-quarters airbrake was preferred during the approach as any increase in airbrake angle resulted in considerable buffeting brought about primarily by the changes in jet pipe geometry from the Buccaneer S.1. Control during the four-degree approach was satisfactory and no difficulties were experienced in maintaining an accurate approach path, or in lining the aircraft up with the centre line.

During the approach it was important to maintain a minimum BLC trailing edge duct pressure of 15 PSI as this provided an adequate margin (approximately 15 knots) over stalling speed, however, should BLC pressure fall to zero, there would be no margin and stalling speed would then equal the datum speed. Shore based tests prior to the trial on HMS *Eagle* had shown that low BLC pressures were likely to be experienced with the 'dovetail' standard engine during approaches at low all-up weights. During the HMS *Eagle* trials some approaches were made high and fast and to correct this, the pilot reduced engine rpm by 2-3 per cent, however this had the effect of reducing BLC pressure to 10-15 PSI which was considered to be rather too close to the stall for comfort. Urgent action was taken after the trial on HMS *Eagle* to investigate ways of improving this situation, either by making changes to the engine, or by altering the airframe so as to increase drag, which would, in turn, lead to increased rpm and greater BLC pressure. Unfortunately no solutions were found that did not require extensive engine and/or airframe modifications, although rescheduling of the inlet guide vanes/bleed valve movements in relation to engine rpm did bring about some improvement. Despite the fact that the BLC pressures were still thought to be below those desirable for Service use, they were considered acceptable for initial carrier release in temperate conditions, providing that a minimum speed of 125 kts IAS was used at all weights below 32,000 lb.

With the Buccaneer S.1, single-engine approaches with BLC on were flown with the configuration set at 30/10/10, however, with the increased thrust of the S.2 it was decided to use 30/20/20 with BLC on as this would allow a reduction of approximately 6 knots in the approach speed due to the use of increased aileron droop. During the deck trials with the S.2 only one simulated single-engine (one engine idling) arrested landing was made, however, much experience was gained during a number of roller landings and overshoots to the extent that the single-engine characteristics of the S.2 were established. Using the 30/20/20 configuration with BLC on and an approach speed 6 knots above the normal two-engine approach speed (133 kts IAS at 33,000 lb) no serious handling or overshoot problems were encountered up to the normal maximum deck landing weight of 35,000 lb.

It was noticed, however, that small changes in rpm and airbrake angle produced yawing movements during the approach, to the point that this made lining up with the deck centre-line more difficult. These difficulties were reduced if the correct approach speed was stabilised early on and this also assisted in the maintenance of adequate BLC pressure as large adjustments of rpm were less likely to be required at late stages in the approach. Rpm on the live engine was usually of the order of 85-89 per cent and this resulted in a BLC pressure of around 15-18 PSI. When on the approach, full rudder trim and a small foot force were required to maintain directional trim, but during the subsequent overshoot when full rpm was selected on the live engine the foot forces increased to moderate to heavy (it was hoped that this would be alleviated by a proposed increase in rudder trim authority).

When approaching on two engines with BLC off, the 45/10/10 configuration with three-quarter airbrake deflection, as used on the Buccaneer S.1, was found to be equally satisfactory for the S.2. To maintain adequate controllability during this type of approach, a speed 12 kts IAS above the normal BLC on speed (i.e 139 kts IAS at 33,000 lb) had to be maintained. Any further reductions in approach speeds were considered undesirable due to reasons of deteriorating lateral control and a reduced margin from the stall. The incidence on the approach was slightly higher than in the normal BLC on condition but the view for landing was still adequate. During an overshoot following a bolter, some increased sensitivity was noted in the pitch control and it was easy to over-rotate when returning to the approach incidence value, particularly if the nosewheel had been allowed to touch the deck.

From the trials carried out on HMS *Eagle* and HMS *Ark Royal* it was recommended that CA release be given for the carrier operation of the Buccaneer S.2 by day or night up to 50,000 lb AUW in ISA conditions. Single engine and BLC off deck landings could be made in an emergency with the appropriate increments above normal approach speeds. The point was made, however, that every effort should be made to provide increased BLC pressure during the deck landing approach, either by the provision of additional airframe drag or by improvements in the engine characteristics.

After its entry into Royal Navy service the Buccaneer S.2 came to be regarded as one of the finest strike aircraft in the world. It also had a reputation of being one of the toughest so it might come as a surprise to many to discover that the aircraft hit fatigue problems as early as 1971. Fatigue cracks were discovered in the engine ring of the front main spar of an 800 Squadron aircraft in October 1971 and very soon three more aircraft (including an RAF machine) were seen to have similar cracks. All affected aircraft had to be grounded, the problem being more critical for the Navy due to the more advanced fatigue life of their aircraft.

As the first aircraft to be discovered with cracks were the fatigue leaders (Fatigue Index 89-97) it was assumed that failures would be unlikely to occur below FI 80 and that this would leave a reasonable amount of time to resolve the problem for the bulk of the fleet. To put this into some sort of perspective, the Buccaneer had at that time been cleared up to FI 180. During April 1972, however, two RAF aircraft were found to be cracked at FI 59 and 65 which indicated that the problem was more far reaching than at first thought. The following month five further aircraft were discovered with cracks, one having a Fatigue Index as low as 47.

Various remedies were proposed to solve the problem of premature fatigue including the fitting of new spar rings with thickened webs. It was considered essential for these to be applied to the seventeen aircraft still to be produced and to those aircraft already cracked, although the means by which this could be carried out was still unclear. Another possible solution was the use of doubling plates, however, these were only suitable as reinforcement for aircraft that were, as yet, unaffected. A cheaper, short term answer lay in stress relief of the affected area. Most of the cracks emanated from holes within the spar ring and as these were not particularly well drilled, it was argued that reaming them out would remove the stress raisers that were causing the cracks. It was also believed that by boring the holes out and pre-stressing them by pushing through an oversized steel ball, there would be sufficient gain which, together with certain flying restrictions, would hold off the worst of the effects until the doubling plates could be brought in.

The flying restrictions were brought in by a Special Flying Instruction (SFI) which limited normal accelerations at various speeds and weights. For example, at the higher end of the Mach range (0.88-0.95 IMN) post Mod.1213 aircraft (strengthened fin) were limited to -2.75 to +3.5g at all-up weights up to 44,000 lb, or -2.75 to +3.0g for pre Mod.1213 aircraft. When operating in the higher weight category (53,000-59,000 lb) the limitations were more severe at -2.0 to +2.5g (post Mod.1213) and -2.0 to +2.0g (pre Mod.1213). Whenever convenient, it was recommended that all heavy stores, such as 1,000 lb bombs, be carried on the wing stations in preference to the bomb bay to further reduce fatigue damage. These limitations at least allowed the Buccaneer to continue flying while long term measures were put in place. This involved replacing the cracked components by new rings of an improved design and the first replacement was carried out by Hawker Siddeley in two weeks, a shorter time than many had envisaged. Although this problem was eventually dealt with, serious fatigue returned to haunt the Buccaneer force at the end of the 1970s (see Chapter Eleven).

In addition to the problems of premature fatigue, in the early 1970s the Buccaneer S.2 was also beset by a number of failures of its Rolls-Royce Spey engines. A reheated version of the Spey had been adopted for the British version of the McDonnell Douglas Phantom and the numbers of engine failures on this aircraft were at worrying levels, so much so that several OCU courses had to be cancelled as there were not enough flying hours available to train new pilots and navigators and maintain Britain's commitment to NATO. The problems with the Buccaneer were not quite as bad as that of the Phantom but the failures were related in that they involved blade fractures of the first stage of the low-pressure compressor (LP1). Initially Rolls-Royce proposed in the short term that Mod.3030, a redesigned 'twisted' blade with a new retaining pin, should be used. In the long term, however, it was recommended that a completely redesigned blade known as a 'clappered' blade should be incorporated.

Several Royal Navy aircraft were fitted with Mod.3030 blades but these failed at a much earlier stage than had been predicted and the modification was quickly withdrawn. As the 'clappered' blade would not be ready until 1973 a number of engine restrictions, primarily concerned with engine handling, were imposed to reduce the stress loading line of the low-pressure compressor. These included avoiding specific rpm bands during ground running and making sure that the engines were not run on the ground for lengthy periods in crosswind or gusty conditions. It was also beneficial if the engines did not ingest the hot gases from other aircraft and in this respect restrictions were put in force to prevent aircraft from taxiing at close intervals. In addition, the spacings during stream take-offs and landings were extended.

Buccaneer squadrons operating in Strike Command and in RAF Germany were also thoroughly briefed on the types of flying manoeuvres that should be avoided. As a result there was a marked reduction in the number of asymmetric overshoots carried out and the trail distances between aircraft using weapons ranges were also extended. Orders were also put out that compass swings were not to be carried out with the engines running. The long suffering ground crews were required to carry out an LP1 blade check after every flight, this operation taking around 1½ hours to complete. A new service repair procedure was established in September 1971 which authorised stations to carry out LP1 blade changes on defective engines and by early 1972 RAF Honington had carried out six such repairs. Eventually the problems experienced with the Spey engine in the Phantom and Buccaneer were overcome and it was made into a reliable engine with acceptable Time Between Overhauls (TBO).

Sadly, the Buccaneer never received the development that would have improved its capability even further. The possibility of overseas sales to the US Navy and the West German *Marineflieger* came to nothing and the only export version was the S.50, of which sixteen were produced in 1965/66 for the South African Air Force (SAAF). This was an adaptation of the basic S.2 which was fitted with two retractable Bristol Siddeley BS.605 twin-chamber rocket engines, each of 4,000 lb thrust, mounted in the rear fuselage. This was to give the South African Buccaneers an adequate safety margin when taking off at gross weight in 'hot and high' conditions, their proposed base at Waterkloof being nearly 5,000 feet above sea level. In the event rocket-assisted take-offs were hardly ever used as runway length was found to be adequate for most operations, with flight refuelling being available as a back-up.

Other variations from the British S.2 included the deletion of the hydraulic wing fold mechanism (the wings could still be folded manually) and an armament of four Nord AS 30 air-to-surface guided missiles. The role of the Buccaneer in South African service was to protect the sea lanes around the Cape of Good Hope, however, this important task was conveniently disregarded by the Labour government led by Harold Wilson which vetoed a follow-up order of another twenty Buccaneers and only reluctantly agreed to the original batch being delivered. This was on the basis that the aircraft could be used for counter-insurgency operations to enforce South Africa's policy of apartheid (the fact that France and Italy were supplying South Africa with aircraft that were much more suited to COIN operations was ignored!).

The Buccaneer had a tough life in SAAF service and by the time that the aircraft was retired in April 1991, only five aircraft remained. Of the in-service losses, three aircraft went down as a result of collisions, two crashed during night exercises and two succumbed to stall/spin accidents. Three more crashed as a result of a double engine flame out, an hydraulic failure and structural damage caused when a 1,000 lb bomb hit an aircraft during release trials (one aircraft was also lost during the delivery flight due to another stall and double flame out). Having been used almost exclusively in the anti-shipping role for its first decade in South African service, the Buccaneer then saw considerable action during the war against Marxist rebels in Angola. Here it proved to be highly suited to the task due to its ability to carry a large amount of weaponry over long ranges. It was also able to remain over the target area for longer than any other aircraft in theatre and could respond with close-air support to a rapidly changing situation on the ground.

As was the case with the Avro Vulcan which saw action during the Falklands war in 1982, the RAF's Buccaneer force also went to war late in its service career, in this case during the 1991 Iraq conflict. Initially the Buccaneer did not figure in the RAF's plans as strike sorties were to be flown exclusively by Tornado GR.1s, backed up by the Jaguar GR.1, however, the vulnerability of the Tornado during low-level attacks against Iraqi airfields led to a rethink and the Buccaneer was suddenly required to fulfil a designation role for Tornado attacks from medium level using 1,000 lb laser guided bombs (LGBs). This led to a period of intense activity at Lossiemouth as an initial batch of six aircraft were prepared for action with the Pave Spike designator, IFF Mode 4, Have Quick II secure radios, the AN/ALQ-101 ECM jamming pod, AIM-9L Sidewinder air-to-air missile and the AN-ALE-40 chaff/flare dispenser, plus a coat of 'desert' pink camouflage paint. These aircraft had arrived at Muharraq by 28 January 1991 (the detachment was increased to twelve shortly afterwards) and the first operational sorties were flown on 2 February.

The first operation involved two Buccaneers providing laser designation, or 'spiking', for Tornado GR.1s of XV Squadron tasked with destroying the Al Suwaira road bridge. The lead aircraft was flown by the boss of the detachment, Wing Commander Bill Cope of 208 Squadron with Flight Lieutenant Carl Wilson in the rear seat. The other aircraft paired Flight Lieutenant Glenn Mason and Squadron Leader Norman Browne. Once over the target the aircraft was put into a dive so that the bridge was acquired in the pilot's head-up display. The Pave Spike was slaved to the sight and when the navigator was satisfied that he had the target on his TV screen, he took over control of the attack which allowed his pilot to climb back to the cruising altitude. The target was then marked by the designator and the laser was fired a few seconds after the Tornadoes had dropped their bombs. The most nerve wracking part of the flight was the wait for the bombs to explode which from a height of 20,000 ft took around 30 seconds. The mission was a complete success, the Buccaneer's long range being highlighted by the fact that only one air-to-air refuelling was needed compared to three by the Tornadoes.

With the non-appearance of the Iraqi Air Force the decision was made to delete the AIM-9L from the Buccaneer's weapons fit which allowed it to carry up to two LGBs which could be self-designated. Having initially concentrated on transportation, particularly bridges, the list of targets was soon extended to include airfields, with hardened aircraft shelters and runways being singled out for attention. Command and control bunkers and military storage depots were also hit. By the end of the war the Buccaneers had flown a total of 216 sorties during which they had assisted in the release of 169 LGBs by Tornadoes and had dropped a further forty-eight themselves. The detachment returned to Lossiemouth on 17 March 1991 having proved that, despite its age, the Buccaneer was still a formidable weapon of war, albeit in a role far different from that for which it had been designed.

CHAPTER NINE

Buccaneer Tactics – Anti-shipping

Although the Buccaneer was designed as a low-level strike aircraft capable of delivering a tactical nuclear weapon against naval targets, it was not long before its role was extended to include the use of conventional weapons. This meant that crews had to become proficient in a large number of attack profiles, the use of which depended on the type of target and its associated defenses, the weapons load they were carrying and the prevailing weather conditions.

The standard nuclear attack profile comprised the LABS manoeuvre, also known as the long toss mode. This involved a high level transit to approximately 200 miles from the target, at which point the observer would identify and mark the target on the Blue Parrot radar before the aircraft descended to sea level to carry out the rest of the run in at 550 kts IAS and 100 ft so as not to be illuminated on the enemy radar screens. The Buccaneer would then be flown on a collision course track, provided that the observer's estimates for target course, speed and the wind velocity were correct. At a range of 4-4¹/₂ miles the aircraft would be pulled up into the first half of a loop at 4-5g during which the onboard computer would automatically work out the release point. Once the weapon had been released a rolling pull-out was made so that the Buccaneer left the target area at low level on a reciprocal course. Although this method of attack required a radar lock, there were no weather limitations. Line errors were in the region of 100-150 feet, although accuracy tended to deteriorate against a manoeuvring target. As the time of flight of the weapon was relatively long and accuracy levels were not that good, this method of attack was not used when carrying conventional stores.

When carrying out missions with conventional weapons a wide range of attack profiles were available. The medium toss mode was the standard conventional toss attack and was similar to that described above, however the pull-up point was much nearer the target and was carried out at a minimum distance of two miles. The type of weapon used for this form of attack was the VT fused 1,000 lb bomb, of which a total of eight could be carried (four internally and four externally). These were released automatically in the climb, the aircraft leaving the target area in the same manner as for long toss delivery. Although accuracy levels were improved compared with the long toss delivery mode, errors within the weapon system meant that the effectiveness of this type of attack with conventional weapons was called into question. Another type of attack to be attempted was known as the locked-on dive toss (LODT). This involved the Buccaneer approaching the target in a shallow dive before a pull-up was initiated when within 8-11 seconds of the target. This was another blind attack which required a radar lock but due to the approach pattern of the aircraft, it was found to be rather more vulnerable to defensive fire. This method was a relatively unreliable type of attack with extremely critical parameters and was not generally used by Royal Navy squadrons.

Other methods of attack utilised a 20 degree dive with around 7.5 degrees of depression of the weapon sight, the release of the bombs being either manual or automatic. With a manual depressed sightline (MDSL) the pilot would track the target through his strike sight with the aiming mark at the required angle of depression and offset to left or right to allow for wind and/or target movement. The bombs would be released at a height of 2,000 ft. This method of weapons release could achieve excellent accuracy although a high level of proficiency was needed on the part of the crew as dive angle, IAS and height were all critical. Due to the high workload involved with this type of attack it was expected that there would be considerable degradation of accuracy during actual operations, however it was likely that this mode would have to be adopted should an aircraft be suffering from equipment unserviceability.

The primary conventional delivery technique that was adopted for Royal Navy use was known as the automatic depressed sightline (ADSL). This was a visual attack (like MDSL) that normally required a cloud base of 4,000 ft although in the case of ADSL a form of low-level attack could be made with a cloud base of only 1,500 ft. The automatic weapons release in ADSL was governed by a signal from the Buccaneer's vertical accelerometer. The attack was carried out in a bunted dive, the pilot once again tracking the target through the strike sight, but in doing so he had to gradually reduce the 'g' loading on the aircraft. When a reading of approximately 0.5g was obtained on the vertical accelerometer, the bombs were released. With a weapon sight depression of 7.5 degrees, this occurred at 2,000 ft and 450 kts IAS. Assuming that all the various parameters had been set correctly, errors of less than 100 ft were soon being obtained by Royal Navy squadrons. As the system compensated for dive angle and IAS errors, the cockpit workload was considerably reduced so that a reasonable level of accuracy was achieved, even by relatively inexperienced crews. The final delivery mode in this series gave automatic release on radar range from a manual dive profile and was referred to in abbreviated form as RRADSL. Range results were extremely encouraging with errors no more than that for ADSL, although problems were experienced with the radar lock.

Conventional bombing attacks using 1,000 lb retarded bombs could also be carried out using a standard laydown technique in which the target was approached at around 200 ft and 500 kts IAS. With this mode, of course, the target had to be acquired visually and the aircraft had to be flown very accurately, especially in terms of height and speed. This was not always easy, particularly if the aircraft was subject to low level turbulence. During trials, laydown attacks proved to be extremely accurate, although problems were experienced with a number of 1,000 lb bombs failing to retard properly. The fact that the Buccaneer had to fly over the target following weapons release also meant that it was susceptible to defensive fire.

The Buccaneer was also cleared for firing 2 in rocket projectiles (RP), thirty-six of which could be housed in up to four underwing pods. These were intended mainly for use against smaller vessels, such as fast patrol boats, and could be ripple fired at one of two speeds. At the faster setting all selected pods fired on a single press of the trigger, whereas during a 'slow ripple', firing only took place during trigger depression. This type of attack was carried out visually from shallow dives and generally resulted in very low errors of around 20-30 ft. The final attack mode for the Buccaneer resembled the LABS manoeuvre and was known as the vari-toss. In this case a Lepus flare was released at a specific point during the pull-up so that it illuminated the target for attack by other aircraft. Although the degree of accuracy was no better than that for a preset LABS manoeuvre, it still represented a more accurate delivery method than a manual release and was more than adequate for illuminating the target so that it could be acquired visually by other aircraft.

By the mid to late 1960s the increased sophistication of Soviet defensive systems meant that the chances of a successful strike with acceptable losses when using conventional 'iron' bombs was becoming less likely. The limitations of the Buccaneer's weapons system for this type of attack were also a concern and there was a pressing need for the introduction of some form of stand-off capability. The first missile system to be tried on the Buccaneer was the US Bullpup air-to-surface missile (ASM) which had been developed in the 1950s following an urgent US Navy requirement which came out of its experiences in the Korean War. Despite extensive trials at Holme-on-Spalding Moor, use of the Bullpup ASM in Royal Navy service was limited due to poor reliability and a basic lack of accuracy.

A more successful missile application, at least as far as the Buccaneer was concerned, was the Martel air-to-surface missile which was developed jointly between Britain and France. This was one of the first European collaborations on a weapons system and involved Hawker Siddeley Dynamics which developed the AJ.168 version of the missile with TV guidance and Matra who were responsible for the AS.37 anti-radar Martel. The name Martel was chosen as it was an abbreviation of Missile Anti-Radar TELevision and both versions had a 330 lb warhead. The AJ.168 TV Martel allowed its operator to monitor the target area via a screen in the cockpit that was fed by a Marconi Space and Defence Systems (MSDS) vidicon camera which was mounted in the nose of the missile. When a target was acquired the TV seeker was locked on before launch. After firing, height was maintained by a barometric lock and the missile was steered by a cockpit-mounted control stick, the video signals from the missile being transmitted to an underwing pod and then to the cockpit display. The anti-radar (AR) version of Martel had a passive radiation seeker which was able to search a pre-set band of frequencies if the exact operating frequency of the enemy radar was not known. Once a lock had been achieved on the target radar, the missile was launched and homing was then carried out automatically. The range of Martel when launched from low level was of the order of seventeen miles and its cruising speed was around Mach 0.90.

The introduction of TV and AR Martel missiles in the mid 1970s radically affected the whole maritime attack concept as they provided a true stand-off capability with a degree of accuracy that had previously not been possible with conventional attacks by the Buccaneer force. Although the new weapon system was a quantum leap in capability, both versions of Martel required that Buccaneer crews be trained to a very high level, even for anti-radar operations, as despite the fact that this missile was a 'launch and leave' system, the workload before launch was extremely high. To assess Martel and to evaluate the tactics for its use, the RAF's Central Tactics and Trials Organisation (CTTO) published a study in June 1974 on the Buccaneer/Martel combination in the counter shipping role.

Based on previous trials it was suggested that the weather minima for TV Martel operations was 4/8 or less cloud with a minimum base of 2,000 ft and a minimum visibility of 3 nm. Normally operations could only be carried out in daylight, i.e. from 30 minutes after sunrise to 30 minutes before sunset, although when operating under clear skies it had already been shown that a ship could be detected some 15 minutes after sunset. In terms of accuracy, TV Martel had achieved its design requirement of an error of no more than 10 ft and it was thought that an error of 20 ft or less should easily be obtained in operational situations. AR Martel was capable of operation in any weather condition, day or night, although its lock-on performance was degraded at times in certain atmospheric conditions.

The TV Martel had a semi-armour piercing warhead which on its first live firing against a target produced a radius of destruction of 30 ft around the impact point. There were some doubts as to the precise aiming points of the various Soviet warships that were the Buccaneer's principal targets. In some cases it was thought best to take out the surface-to-surface missile (SSM) installation, but on the 'Krivak' type destroyer these were mounted in an exposed position near the bows and might well result in a miss. In this case it was recommended that the missile should be aimed at the most substantial area to be presented which was generally amidships, just above the water line. This recommendation also applied if the aiming point was obscured by target movement or by weather conditions. It was also thought that aiming at the waterline in an attempt at a sinking could result in the missile falling short.

The warhead of the AR Martel was triggered either by a proximity or impact fuse and the blast was sufficient to cause severe damage to a radar aerial out to a distance of 30 ft. Although the missile was designed to destroy or significantly degrade a ship's primary surveillance radar, some peripheral damage to superstructure or adjacent equipment was also likely to occur. Such an attack would not be without warning, however, as the Buccaneer at 200 ft would have been detected by passive intercept of its Blue Parrot radar at about 30 nm or by the surveillance radars at about 25 nm (radar horizon) well before the maximum AR Martel low level firing range which was 16-17 nm.

When considering the operational aspects of TV Martel it was discovered that, in most light conditions, attacking into sun produced the highest contrast levels between ships and the sea surface, the resulting silhouette standing out well on the TV screen. A beam-on approach enhanced the silhouette effect, thus permitting earlier detection and identification and offering the best choice of aiming points. Other factors affecting the detection range included the size and type of the target and the relationship between sea state and target speed. The wake of the ship was readily visible on the TV screen and, in conditions of good visibility, might be seen by the pilot even before missile launch. Soviet warships did have the capability to lay a smoke screen which could obscure aiming points, although a period of time was needed to effect this defence and the use of smoke could work in the attackers favour as it could assist in the early acquisition of an individual ship or a Surface Action Group (SAG).

One of the likely problems with TV Martel, as identified by CTTO, was the attainment of an accurate launch point. Once the target had been acquired, some three minutes were required for the missile's gyro slaving and arming sequences, during which the Buccaneer was restricted in the manoeuvres it could carry out, with limits being imposed in terms of rate of turn and heading changes. For an approach speed of 420 kts IAS, this sequence had to be initiated some 38 nm from the target if the missile was to be launched at its maximum range of 17.5 nm. This posed problems in terms of target acquisition and range estimation, whilst restricting the degree of tactical manoeuvre available and reducing the element of surprise because of the need for earlier use of the Blue Parrot radar. If launch range was reduced, these difficulties were lessened and there were several other advantages. The shorter time of flight meant that launch alignment errors were reduced and there was less time for the missile to be engaged by the target defences. As the terminal phase was executed with the missile motor still operating there was also excellent target penetration which increased the missile's destructive capabilities.

TV Martel had been designed to adopt a cruise height of 2,000 ft but during release to service trials there had been a distinct lack of consistency in this respect. Of the eighteen missiles fired successfully, only five settled at the correct height, the remaining thirteen cruising randomly high or low by up to 1,000 ft, although the mean error was about 300 ft. The missile had a height step-down function which enabled cloud to be avoided or a high cruise height to be corrected, but this also proved to be troublesome, the missile, on occasions, regaining its original height after a down-step had been selected. After launching of the missile, the Buccaneer began its post launch manoeuvre (PLM) which at a launch speed of 420 kts IAS took it about 2-3 nm closer to the target. If a maximum range profile had been adopted a slight climb to about 500 ft was necessary along the withdrawal heading so that the data link was maintained up to missile impact. Despite this it was considered that the climb would not decrease the Buccaneer's chances of survival.

The AR version of Martel came with two types of detector head so, to achieve the maximum possible cover, two missiles, each with a different detector head, would be carried. These were able to detect the primary maritime surveillance radars, although neither could pick up the Soviet Fire Control Radars (FCRs). During initial trials an intermittent but usable lock-on was achieved at ranges in excess of the radar horizon and positive lock always occurred before the aircraft could normally be detected by a fully alerted radar operator in a target ship. Initial clearance for AR Martel was for it to be launched at low level only, although ultimately it was hoped that release heights of up to 35,000 ft would be included. It was felt that determining the actual location of the radar source to which the missile had locked would be the greatest problem with AR Martel as the only information that was available from the missile itself was the bearing and frequency of the emission. The approximate range therefore had to be estimated based on the nature of the lock, the calculated range of the radar horizon at the time and the probable height of the target aerial. Because the detector head achieved lock-on beyond maximum missile range at all heights, the aircraft radar had to be used to determine firing opportunities.

The use of AR Martel also offered the opportunity of the so-called 'run-pairs' facility in which two AR missiles carried on either the two inboard or two outboard stations were simultaneously armed, although only one missile on a selected station could be locked to its target and fired. The 'run-pairs' facility also extended to a mix of one AR and one TV missile, provided that the TV missile was selected first and remained so up to launch. This particular option was not available when an ECM pod was fitted, however, as this was carried on the port outer station and the data link pod for TV Martel could only be fitted to an inboard station.

As well as assessing the missile system itself, CTTO also looked at how Martel could best be used, together with the other options that were still available to the Buccaneer force. The arrival of Martel into service in 1972/73 caused as many problems as it solved in that it added to the multiplicity of roles and attack modes that had to be fulfilled by a limited number of aircraft. Consideration also had to be given to the poor overworked Buccaneer navigator, particularly during the critical attack phase. In some instances he may well have been in serious danger of overload in having to operate TV and/or AR Martel, at the same time as managing a secondary bombing attack, the ECM pod and the passive warning receiver (PWR). This, of course, was in addition to his normal duties of navigation, attack co-ordination and monitoring functions. In an attempt to keep the workload within manageable levels it was recommended that aircraft be fitted with either TV or AR Martel, but not both.

Another reason for avoiding a mix of TV and AR Martel on individual aircraft was the fact that only four underwing stations were available. Assuming that two would be taken up by ECM and data link pods, this left the other two for the missiles. As two AR missiles were required to take out the 'Topsail' and 'Headnet' surveillance radars that were associated with most primary targets, it made sense to employ one aircraft to do this, while the rest of the strike force employed TV Martel. Where range and all-up weight considerations permitted, a valuable back-up to Martel was the addition of four 1,000 lb bombs in each bomb bay of attacking aircraft, as follow-up visual bombing attacks were far less vulnerable against defences already degraded by the initial Martel attack.

When selecting the type of attack that was to be used for daylight operations an important factor was the weather conditions prevalent in the target area. At the time that TV Martel entered service the deciding factors as to its use in terms of cloud base and visibility were 2,000 ft and 3 nm respectively. AR Martel and medium toss bombing deliveries were possible in all weather conditions and so represented the sole attack modes that could be contemplated when visibility was less than 3 nm and the cloud base was less than 2,000 ft. When visibility was above 3 nm but cloud base was below 2,000 ft this opened up the possibility of carrying out laydown or 10 degree dive attacks which were more accurate than the medium toss mode, but were distinctly more vulnerable to defensive fire. With no visibility or cloud base restrictions, all attack modes were possible, i.e. TV Martel, laydown, 10/20 degree dive attacks, medium toss and AR Martel. For operations at night unrestricted use of medium toss and AR Martel was available. All the visual attack modes required the use of illumination, usually by Lepus flares, but target acquisition problems favoured dive attacks as the shadow of the target cast on the surface of the sea, or the wake of a target moving at speed, could not easily be scanned in flight at low levels.

The effectiveness of a bombing attack depended very much on the mode used, but in general terms the more accurate the attack, the more vulnerable was the Buccaneer to defensive fire from the target. Good hit probabilities were usually obtained from laydown, 10 and 20 degree dive attacks, whilst the accuracy achieved from medium toss deliveries (at least in the mid 1970s) was generally poor. The former attacks were extremely vulnerable to AAA and SA-N-4 which was the standard short-range surface-to-air missile (SAM) system of the Soviet Navy. Medium toss aircraft were vulnerable only to SA-N-4 and even this threat was minimised by a shorter exposure time and the ability to carry out evasive manoeuvres. Aircraft engaged on TV Martel operations were invulnerable to the target defences although theoretically the missile could be detected and acquired by defensive radars and was therefore capable of being shot down by AAA and SA-N systems. Perhaps the most dangerous operation as far as the Buccaneer was concerned was the delivery of Lepus flares at night, as during vari-toss or level release the aircraft was highly vulnerable to both AAA and all forms of SA-N missile defences.

The choice of which attack mode to adopt was a tricky one and the balance between the urgency of the task and an acceptable aircraft loss rate was crucial. Where a target had to be attacked without delay and at all costs, the most accurate mode had to be used regardless of vulnerability. However, the maritime Buccaneer force was relatively small and so could not sustain high attrition rates. In view of this, if the Buccaneer had had to go to war for real, some form of compromise would have been made between the swift accomplishment of the task and the associated aircraft losses.

For daylight operations the ability of TV Martel to achieve the required damage levels, whilst the launch aircraft remained invulnerable, dictated that it should be adopted as the primary attack weapon where light and weather conditions allowed. Where TV Martel attacks were not possible, it was recommended by CTTO that the aim should be to use medium toss attacks against the primary target, with 10 degree dive and laydown attacks only being attempted when the operational situation demanded accuracy regardless of loss.

For attacks at night the denial of optical tracking to the close defences was more than counter-balanced by the inability of the attacking force to co-ordinate sufficient aircraft to saturate the target's defences. Night attack was particularly difficult as the Lepus and visual attack profiles were complex and both needed to be co-ordinated closely. The positioning of the flares was critical for adequate illumination and this was not an easy task, especially as the Lepus delivery aircraft, although tossing the flares from a distance of about 2 nm, spent much longer in the SA-N-4 engagement envelope than, for example, during a medium toss bomb delivery. The Buccaneer force was also tasked with attacks against fast patrol boats (FTBs) where the defences were of a much lower order, and in these cases Lepus flares were used to illuminate the boats for an attack by aircraft carrying two in RP.

When carrying out conventional bombing attacks, in order to achieve the required damage levels it was necessary to saturate the defences to the extent that sufficient weapons reached the target. To do this, co-ordinated attacks were made by formations of Buccaneers. These involved up to eight aircraft with a mix of attack modes being adopted, the first using the relatively invulnerable toss mode to soften up the target's defensive capability before the second wave struck with highly vulnerable, but more accurate visual attacks. Such co-ordinated attacks were easy to get wrong, especially in times of war, and so constant practice was needed to maintain aircrew proficiency. For examples of these types of conventional attacks see Figs 1 and 2.

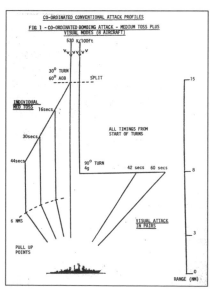

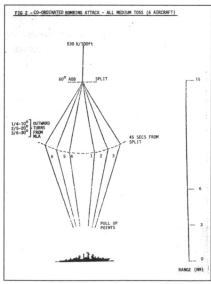

The approach to the target was characterised by uncertainties as to the position of the primary target which then needed to be positively identified. During exercises the attack direction had often been given to the Buccaneer force by airborne early warning (AEW) Shackletons. This had proved to be a highly successful method of target designation as accurate information was continually available on the position of the target relative to the attack formation. In wartime, however, the use of the very small AEW Shackleton force in this role, at the expense of its primary air defence task, appeared doubtful. Furthermore, the procedure relied on freedom from voice or radar jamming. An alternative was the use of a Canberra as a visual probe but it was felt that the information obtained would not be accurate enough for the attacking Buccaneers. This left the possibility of using a 'probe' Buccaneer to penetrate the target area until radar burn-through was achieved or visual contact was made with the actual target. Although a bearing could well be obtained, the actual range of the attacking force from the target was another matter and depending on the level of electronic jamming, co-ordinated mixed mode attacks occasionally had to be abandoned.

The final approach to the target needed to be made at a height of 200 ft or less so that the Buccaneers remained beneath the minimum effective height of Soviet SA-N-1 Goa and SA-N-3 Goblet missile systems. Speed was no real protection against the short range defences (SA-N-4 and AAA) and tended to work against the attacking force in several respects. The cockpit workload, which was already high, was increased still further and flying at higher speeds also increased fuel consumption. In addition, the amount of black smoke being emitted from the exhausts was also increased, which could give away the Buccaneer's position, and cockpit noise levels were higher. Until acceleration was essential for a particular attack mode, it was recommended that the low-level penetration speed be limited to 420 kts IAS which was also the aircraft's best turning speed. This meant that the Buccaneer could carry out effective evasion should the passive warning radar indicate that it had been illuminated by the FCR of a ship other than the intended target.

In an attempt to achieve surprise it was normal practice to maintain RT silence, to use elaborate descent profiles and to employ a weave approach at low level, whilst delaying the switch-on of the radar until 25 nm from the estimated position of the target. Despite all these techniques it was the conclusion of CTTO that they were unlikely to succeed against the sophisticated Soviet electronic equipment available to both the target and to any outlying picket ships. Indeed the target may have already been alerted by the activities of AEW Shackletons or visual probe aircraft. The key to a successful attack was an accurate approach with all the defensive aids operational to minimise the effects of electronic jamming. To this end, the

Blue Parrot radar had to be used cautiously in an attempt to clarify ship dispositions and to mark the target whenever target area intelligence was suspect. Multiple aircraft attacks, particularly where aircraft were spaced radially on the attack run, tended to reduce the effectiveness of jamming on any one Blue Parrot radar, but the jamming of voice communications could well be sufficient to disrupt any but the simplest attempts at co-ordination. During the final run in to the target, use of the ECM pod was essential to provide some level of protection against engagement by Soviet FCRs.

The co-ordinated, mixed mode attack was extremely difficult to carry out as it could easily be affected by navigational inaccuracies, target location and identification difficulties, timing, weather and ECM. In situations where a Martel attack was not possible, CTTO were of the opinion that medium toss should be the primary bombing mode as this offered the best chance of success, coupled with the conservation of the Buccaneer force for future operations. It was estimated that the chances of success for a co-ordinated medium toss attack by four aircraft, each carrying six 1,000 lb bombs, against a single ship would be between 34 per cent and 54 per cent. With six aircraft taking part the success rate went up to between 50 per cent and 68 per cent.

As with visual bombing, when using Martel it was important to try to saturate the defences by co-ordinated multiple attacks. This was due to the fact that TV Martel missiles could only be launched and guided singly, and so they were vulnerable to all the target defences. By firing multiple missiles over a short time span the chances of at least one Martel hitting the target was virtually ensured. For ease of handling a Martel attack formation, it was felt by CTTO that it should generally consist of four aircraft plus an Attack Director. A large number of combinations of TV and AR missile attacks were possible, however, three were considered as follows

2 TV and 2 AR
2 TV and 2 x 2 AR (run-pairs)
4 TV

It was considered that the best overall probability of success lay with the simultaneous launch of four TV missiles. The important part to be played in the radar suppression role by AR Martel was recognised and it was recommended that two AR missiles be carried on the aircraft flown by the Attack Director. This would either force the ship target to maintain radar silence or suffer damage to its radar installation. So as to cause confusion within the enemy defences it was best for the AR attack to come from a different direction to that of the TV Martel attack.

Any Martel attack would invariably have come under the influence of

Soviet ECM. The use of Blue Parrot for target marking was likely to prompt jamming which would deny target range information. Burn-through against the Soviet jammers was unlikely to occur before reaching the TV or AR missile launch points and so the target had to be marked at the start of the run in, using a few sweeps of Blue Parrot, before spot jamming became effective. Provided accurate target marking was achieved, subsequent jamming was ineffective in preventing a TV Martel attack, the Target Marker Computer (TMC) providing adequate range information and the missile data link being virtually immune to interference.

At the time that the CTTO report was written Martel had only just entered service so suitable tactics had not been formulated, however, a strong case was put forward for an Attack Director to be responsible for overall attack co-ordination. His functions would be to provide the position, disposition and positive identification of the target and to maintain an overall appreciation of the tactical situation before, during and after the Martel attack. To accomplish this he was to operate as a probe by detaching from the attack formation at a range of some 100 nm from the target's position. Although the Director would be spending more time in the target area than the rest of the Buccaneers it was thought that as a single aircraft, its manoeuvrability, combined with effective use of the PWR and ECM pod, would confer reasonable immunity.

Having identified the target, the Attack Director was in a good position to be able to specify the ideal attack direction with regard to target course, light conditions and the defence threat and he was also able to provide a diversionary influence. More importantly, his presence was likely to compel the Soviet forces to use their surveillance radars which made them vulnerable to an attack by AR Martel. Although in one respect it was best for the Attack Director's aircraft to have a limited weapon load for increased manoeuvrability, the carriage of at least two AR missiles would enable him to attack the surveillance radars in advance of the TV missile attack. Any local surprise that might have been possible would, of course, have been sacrificed.

The TV Martel attack formation was to establish itself in a holding pattern at a position decided by the Attack Director, but normally some 60-70 nm from the target. At this stage the formation would be flying at a height of 200 ft or below with Blue Parrot radars set to standby. On being called in by the Attack Director, the formation spread itself on a broad front towards the target, with a spacing of 1-2 nm between individual aircraft. To achieve initial marking by Blue Parrot before there was a serious threat of spot jamming, the formation had to make a simultaneous pop-up above 200 ft for one or two radar sweeps of the target, before descending again to low level.

The recommended attack speed was 420 kts IAS which allowed an effective break to be made should the PWR indicate an imminent threat from any outlying ships that were protecting the main target. It also endowed a high level of turn performance during the post launch manoeuvre to keep the Buccaneer out of the target's short-range defences. The attack height was 200 ft which was the minimum for TV missile launch and also provided immunity from SA-N-1 and SA-N-3 surface-to-air missiles. If other ships provided a threat during the run in to the launch point, however, the approach could be made below the 200 ft missile release height.

The optimum distance bracket for the launch of TV Martel was 8-10 nm which decreased the chances of acquisition by defensive radars and limited the number of SA-N missiles that could be fired against it. To achieve this, the gyro slaving and missile arming cycle had to be started at a minimum range of 31 nm. To resolve any error in target position, particularly if the primary target was in a group of ships, it was recommended that Blue Parrot be used again for target marking prior to the arming cycle when range to the target was estimated to be 40 nm. This should have ensured confirmation of the target before range had been reduced to 31 nm.

The start of the arming cycle coincided with penetration of the target's surveillance radar lobe and it was likely that the Buccaneer would be detected at this range. Using a launch range of 8-10 nm, however, the aircraft would remain clear of the SA-N-4 and AAA defensive zones during the PLM, even allowing for a possible 20 per cent error in the launch range. The facility to break away in either direction during the PLM regardless of the data link pod station, increased flexibility during the recovery phase and allowed a rapid withdrawal from the target area.

As most of the primary targets were fitted with two surveillance radars it was best for the Attack Director to carry at least two AR missiles, so that a search could be made for both radars using the run-pairs facility. An intermittent detector head lock-on was normally obtained at a target range of 25-30 nm, allowing the missile to be launched in a range bracket of 12-15 nm. If his primary attack direction duties permitted, the Attack Director was to attempt to fire his AR missiles to ensure that they arrived at the target immediately prior to the launch of the TV missiles. Ideally he would also have used an attack direction different to that of the main formation so as to cause the maximum confusion to the enemy defences. After launch, the Attack Director was not inhibited by any missile control function and was free to adopt a flight profile that would serve to heighten the amount of confusion among the Soviet defences (for a co-ordinated Martel attack profile see Fig 3).

Although Martel endowed the Buccaneer force with an enhanced capability, it suffered from a number of limitations which took on a greater significance with the rapid improvement of defensive systems in the 1970/80s. As its effective range was only around 10 nm, the parent Buccaneer had to fly relatively close to the intended target which put it in danger from outlying ships. Further disadvantages were that only one missile could be fired at a time as the navigator had to guide it onto the target and as it was not a 'sea-skimming' missile, with the passage of time it became increasingly vulnerable. By 1976 Hawker Siddeley Dynamics (soon to be part of BAe) had begun work on a replacement ASM which was to be produced as the Sea Eagle. This was an extremely advanced weapon and was powered by a Microturbo TRI-60 turbojet of 787 lb.s.t. instead of the solid propellant rocket motor as used on Martel. It had an operational range of 60 nm and was a 'fire-and-forget' weapon as it did not need any assistance from the parent aircraft after launch.

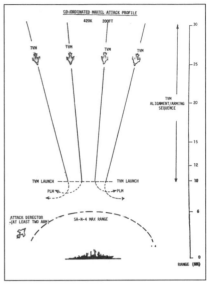

The introduction of Sea Eagle in 1986 offered a vast improvement in capability at the same time as drastically reducing the potential loss rates of the Buccaneer force. A co-ordinated Sea Eagle strike would typically consist of six Buccaneers (each carrying four missiles) which would then split into two sections of three before attacking from different directions. Due to the vastly increased range of Sea Eagle compared to Martel and the fact that it was an autonomous system, the Buccaneers could withdraw immediately after launching their missiles. Unlike Martel, Sea Eagle was a 'sea-skimming' missile which only deviated briefly from its cruise height of around 10 ft to climb to select its target. Having done so, it then descended once again and remained at this height until hitting its target. The aim of the strike was to saturate the defences and in a properly co-ordinated attack, twenty-four missiles would be delivered in a ten second period. As Sea Eagle could be programmed to attack specific targets, such an attack could engage the key elements of a Surface Attack Group whilst ignoring less important ships within the SAG. Due to the fact that it could operate entirely on its own, Sea Eagle was just as effective by night as it was by day. Following its introduction to service with 208 Squadron at Lossiemouth at the end of 1986, Sea Eagle took over as the primary ASM for anti-ship operations and carried on in this role until the Buccaneer was retired in March 1994.

Buccaneer Tactics –
Overland Strike

A lthough the Buccaneer was without doubt one of the finest low-level attack aircraft in the world, the shortcomings of its navigation system imposed limitations on both maritime and limited overland operations and these resulted in numerous studies and proposed modifications to equipment and techniques. The Buccaneer's inadequacies in this respect were highlighted even more when the aircraft was introduced into RAF service in 1969 in the overland strike role. In 1970 the RAF's Central Tactics and Trials Organisation (CTTO) based at High Wycombe in Buckinghamshire carried out a tactical study of the Buccaneer which examined the navigation fit at that time. It also quantified the aircraft's capability when it first entered RAF service.

The basic components of the Buccaneer navigation system comprised a Master Reference Gyro, Blue Jacket (Doppler/GPI), TACAN, a Decca roller map, the Blue Parrot radar, an Air Data Computer and a radio altimeter. In simple terms, the Master Reference Gyro (MRG) system provided the aircraft with a stable platform in the horizontal and vertical planes, but the heading read-out for the MRG navigation display was approximately 9 degrees to every quarter of an inch which made accurate initial alignment and steering difficult. Additional errors also affected the heading display with the result that the MRG was nowhere near as accurate as an inertial system.

Blue Jacket was a pulsed Doppler system incorporating a ground position indicator (GPI). It provided displays of dead reckoning (DR) position, track and groundspeed, or system wind velocity. The equipment was designed to operate over an altitude range of 150-60,000 ft, but experience had shown that the system had a tendency to unlock on many occasions below 300 ft, depending upon terrain or sea state. Switching on or resetting the GPI could cause the position counters to jump by up to 2 nm in GRID mode or 6 minutes of Latitude/Longitude (LAT/LONG), due to the electrical transmission system. There was no storage facility for resetting. The Decca Mk.III roller map was driven by Blue Jacket via a coupling unit and provided a continuous indication of present DR position on a strip map of either ¼ or ½ million scale. This allowed the use of a strip map 568 x 17 nm for ¹/₂ million or 1136 x 34 nm for ¹/₂ million charts.

The Blue Parrot radar could be used to detect targets up to an absolute maximum range of 240 nm, depending upon aircraft height. Scales selectable on the cathode ray tube (CRT) in nautical miles were 0-15, 0-30, 0-60, 0-180 and 60-240. A target marker could be positioned over a radar target either by movement of the Control Radar Set 'joystick', or by means of the range and bearing controls on the Control Indicator (CI). Left and right demands were fed to the Pilot's Display Unit (PDU), and accurate correction demands were displayed when the target was within +/- 7¹/₂ degrees of the aircraft's fore-and-aft axis. Range information was also displayed when the target was 12 nm or less from the aircraft. The radar could also be used to obtain a fix, using controls on the CI which enabled the navigator to obtain slant range and bearing from a recognisable land feature on the radar screen. Positions could be obtained on a 0-50 mile scale or 0-250 mile scale selectable on the CI.

At the time that the Buccaneer entered RAF service the radar picture was of a relatively low standard. The pulse length of the Blue Parrot radar was 2 micro-seconds and the beamwidth was approximately 3 degrees. The resulting Plan Position Indicator (PPI) resolution rectangle at 10 nm on the ¹/₄ million (0-15) scale for a point target was 1,198 yards across track by 465 yards along track. To be able to use the radar for precise map reading when overland, the navigator had to be able to determine his position at all times to within around 2 nm. By making use of the roller map, the navigator had a continuous display of DR position, so that an immediate comparison between radar picture and map could be made. At the time that the CTTO report into the Buccaneer was drafted a navigation technique known as continuous mosaic radar prediction (CMRP) was being developed. This involved the use of radar prediction strips for a particular route which could then be compared with the actual picture on the radar screen. The system was not particularly flexible and involved a high cockpit workload but early trials showed that, once mastered, it worked well enough.

Other aids in the Buccaneer were of limited or no value as far as low level navigation was concerned. The TACAN system gave distance and bearing from a ground station and in general terms was the military equivalent of the civil VOR/DME. As it was a UHF aid, it thus operated on the line of sight principle and so was of little value to an aircraft that spent much of its time at a height of around 250 ft or less. The automatic pilot offered nothing as an operational aid as it was not cleared for use below 400 ft AGL and could not be relied upon for turns greater than 30 degrees below 1,000 ft.

The navigator was able to see strip presentations of True Airspeed and Height from outputs of the Air Data Computer. True Airspeed commenced at

200 knots and was indicated in 10 knot intervals (Indicated Airspeed could be noted by reading the pilot's precision airspeed indicator on the front cockpit to the left of the PDU). Height was poorly presented on a very small scale and was calibrated to standard atmospheric conditions which could not be adjusted. The pilot could obtain accurate height information from a Mk.7B radio altimeter which had two scales, 0-500 ft and 0-5,000 ft, and a variable datum light display system.

In view of the shortcomings of the Buccaneer's navigation fit, a number of modifications were proposed in the early 1970s to improve its capability. The MRG was modified to allow more accurate alignment with a ground datum mark and a replacement GPI maintained its lock down to 80 ft AGL. An improvement to the Blue Parrot radar was known as Monopulse Resolution Enhancement (MRE) which effectively halved the beamwidth to $1\frac{1}{2}$ degrees. The result was that the PPI resolution rectangle at 10 nm range of a point source on the $\frac{1}{4}$ million radar scale was reduced to 664 yards across track by 465 yards along track. This improved performance greatly assisted the use of the radar in conjunction with CMRP strip maps. On modified aircraft the navigator also benefited from having a Combined Speed Indicator (CSI) in the rear cockpit which displayed both indicated and true airspeeds. IAS was displayed by a pointer from 80-800 knots, whilst TAS appeared in digital form from 200 to 700 knots. An altimeter, similar to the pilot's main altimeter, was also fitted.

For Buccaneer squadrons based in Germany the attack profile was flown at low level throughout, with UK based units carrying out a high-level transit before letting down for a low level penetration. High- and medium-level navigation was normally performed using the GPI as the primary aid, backed up by Blue Parrot and TACAN depending on the area of operation and the tactical situation. With modified aircraft, the GPI could be reset as fixes were obtained from the other aids. If the descent was carried out in IMC it was recommended that a coastal penetration be made whenever possible, in order that the low level part of the sortie could be commenced after an accurate fix. Assuming a prominent coastal feature was selected as a fix point, by using the radar it should have been possible to navigate to within $+/-\frac{1}{2}$ nm of this point. The economical cruising speed for the Buccaneer at low level was 420 kts IAS and for most missions the low level cruise phase was flown at this speed. As most visual navigation was practised down to 250 ft AGL, this height was adopted as the normal penetration height, although many crews flying actual operations would have attempted to fly lower than this.

Although the Buccaneer was an excellent aircraft for visual low-level operations, fix monitoring had to be carried out by the crew so that if instrument conditions were encountered, the navigator had accurate error corrections available to apply to the GPI and roller map positions, in order to obtain a reasonably accurate 'real' position. A working party set up to assess the Buccaneer had already stated that it was essential for track-keeping to be maintained at +/-1 nm so that the crew would have a reasonable chance of visually acquiring fix-points, initial points (IPs) and typical targets. To maintain this level of track-keeping accuracy in IMC a fix was required every 37 nm, which at 420 kts IAS was every 5.3 minutes, reducing to 4 minutes at an attack speed of 550 kts IAS. It had been calculated, however, that the practical maximum that a navigator could be expected to maintain under operational conditions was a fix every 7-8 minutes. The reluctant conclusion was thus made that with its existing navigation fit, the Buccaneer was not capable of operating complete sorties in the low level penetration role in instrument conditions.

With aircraft incorporating the modified navigation suite, however, the need to obtain a position fix was reduced and the desired track could be flown within the +/-1 nm error if a fix was calculated every 69 nm. This distance was covered in 9.85 minutes at normal cruise speed and 7.5 minutes at attack speed. The improved nav/attack system thus provided the navigator with a more accurate DR position which did not need to be updated as often and reduced his workload to slightly more manageable levels. At the time of the CTTO report the modifications had not been fully evaluated but service testing was to show sufficient improvement for the Buccaneer to be declared suitable for operations in instrument conditions.

The tactical study carried out by CTTO also included an appreciation of Soviet air defence capability and an assessment of how the Buccaneer would cope against the likely opposition. During an offensive mission over northern Europe low flying Buccaneers could be engaged by defensive fighters, SAM sites and AAA batteries at any time, although in general, specific targets were protected by SAM and AAA, with fighters being used for area defence. The Buccaneer's main asset was its ability to fly at high speed at ultra low level (100 ft or less) which meant that all the component parts of the Soviet defences had to operate under very difficult engagement conditions.

In 1970 the most numerous type of fighter used by Warsaw Pact forces for air defence was the MiG-21 Fishbed with the older D and F models operating alongside smaller numbers of the newer H and J. It was also possible that Buccaneers would come up against the twin-engined Yak-25 Firebar which had entered Soviet Air Force service in the early 1960s. Intelligence estimates on the abilities of these fighters had concluded that none would be very effective below 3,000 ft when operating in IMC and aircraft penetrating in these conditions would be virtually invulnerable to attack by fighters below 1,000 ft. When operating in visual conditions it was, however, a different matter.

In VMC it was expected that defending fighters would operate Combat Air Patrols (CAPs) and then be guided to the general area of a penetrating raid by GCI. This form of control would be based on information received from early warning and surveillance radars, together with reports from ground based observers. Having been vectored towards the threat, the fighters would then have to acquire their targets visually and endeavour to manoeuvre into a descending pursuit curve, aiming for a missile engagement position approximately ½ to 1½ miles behind the intended target at an angle off of 20-30 degrees from the tail. Engagement would normally be made with AA-2 Atoll infra-red (IR) missiles with the possibility of a follow-up cannon attack if the fighter was gun equipped.

The Fishbed D and F both carried two Atoll air-to-air missiles (AAMs) and had a limiting IAS of 595 knots. The newer Fishbed H and J models, which in 1970 were available in small numbers, carried the most up to date version of Atoll, plus a semi-internal, twin-barrel GSh-23L cannon of 23 mm calibre. The earlier MiG-21 variants could also carry this weapon but in a drag-inducing external gun pack. Due to the reduction in drag of the internal gun installation it was estimated that the limiting IAS of Fishbed H was in the region of 650 knots. During low level penetration missions over northern Europe there was a distinct possibility that Buccaneers would have to contend with semi-active radar homing (SARH) versions of Atoll and the AA-3 Anab A as carried by the Yak-25 Firebar. The likelihood of a successful low level interception using this type of AAM was considered to be small, however, due to clutter on the radar screen when illuminating aircraft flying close to the ground. The major fighter threat to Buccaneers at low level was therefore considered to be the IR Atoll fired by Fishbed, to a lesser extent the IR version of Anab (known as Anab B) as carried by Firebar, and follow-up gun attacks (in the early 1970s the Sukhoi Su-15 Flagon and MiG-23 Flogger were entering operational service but these were not considered in the CTTO report as not enough information was known for an accurate assessment of their capabilities to be made).

It was normal Soviet practice to use fighters in pairs with the number two flying a trail position of 1-2,000 yards behind the leader during the attack phase. In these circumstances the fighter crews would almost certainly not be using the on-board AI radar, instead they would be using visual means to put their aircraft into a position where the IR seekers could obtain a firing lock on the target. In the absence of any radar transmission during the final stages of an interception the passive warning radar equipment fitted to some Buccaneers would provide no warning of fighters approaching, or the launch of Atoll missiles (as of 1970 not all Buccaneers were equipped with PWR). It was also thought that AI radar transmission time for fighters being vectored under GCI control had been cut to the absolute minimum. As far as the Buccaneers were concerned it was imperative that low-level penetration formations be optimised for the visual search for fighters and that a good all-round look-out was maintained at all times.

Should a Soviet fighter be seen moving in from behind there were a number of options available to the Buccaneer crew. In terms of speed it was best either to fly at a speed in excess of the limiting IAS of the fighter, or if this was not possible, a good tactic was to decelerate suddenly to a much lower speed. This was readily achieved on the Buccaneer thanks to its extremely powerful airbrakes. A turning target would also make a successful IR Atoll interception difficult and this would be compounded by the target aircraft reducing its IR emission.

A fully loaded Buccaneer could not out-run any of the Fishbed series of aircraft but it stood a better chance of success against a Firebar which had a maximum IAS at sea level of 515 knots. If a Buccaneer was being operated in the clean configuration, however, there was a possibility that it could outpace the earlier MiG-21s if the 580 knot limitation was exceeded for a short period. It was believed that the 595 knot limitation on the Fishbed D and F was a speed that had never to be exceeded and so if a Buccaneer could match it there was little chance of it being intercepted from a stern chase position (in ideal conditions and in the clean configuration, a Buccaneer could be pushed to a speed of just over 600 kts IAS but at any speed above 550 kts IAS there was a gradual deterioration in directional stability due to the build up of shock waves on the wing which then came into contact with the rudder). With the increased low level IAS of the more advanced Fishbed H and J models it was believed that under no circumstances could a Buccaneer out-run this type of aircraft. As already mentioned, a sudden deceleration was also a useful form of evasion but the timing had to be right and the manoeuvre had to be carried out during the critical phase of an Atoll launch.

The chances of a fighter attaining a satisfactory launch position were also reduced if a high 'g' turn was made. If possible it was best for the target aircraft to manoeuvre towards the sun as Atoll performance was considerably degraded if the target could take up a position within 20 degrees of the sun. If missile launch was imminent anything that reduced the Buccaneer's IR emission would reduce the chances of an Atoll kill. This could be achieved by throttling back, extending the airbrakes, turning towards the sun or taking advantage of even partial cloud cover.

It was impossible to be precise on exactly what action to take when a fighter was seen to be closing into an engagement position as factors such as terrain, weather, aircraft weight and the type of interceptor that the Buccaneer was up against all affected the final decision. For any successful disengagement from attacking fighters, however, there were three basic pre-requisites. The Buccaneer pilot had to be completely familiar with the high speed, low-level handling characteristics and limitations of his aircraft, and the fighters had to be seen as early as possible. It was also imperative that the Buccaneer stay as low as possible as there was absolutely nothing to be gained in trying to pull up and turn with a Soviet fighter.

If fighters were visually detected at a range of 2 to 3 miles, by this stage in an interception they would probably have had a reasonable closing speed and it would have been too late to attempt to out-run them. The immediate action in this situation was thus to turn as hard as possible towards the fighters, whilst staying at low level. Should the fighters overshoot, they would probably then pull up into a high speed yo-yo manoeuvre which, if timed correctly, would bring them back down onto the tail of the target, possibly into a gun-firing position. The best defence under these circumstances was to turn towards the fighters once again and maintain a high speed, low level weave, always attempting to turn into any new threat. It was considered vital that even if the fighters made three or four passes, the Buccaneer should stay low and fly as fast as possible. As high speed flight at low levels used up prodigious quantities of fuel, it was probable that the Soviet fighters, which having already spent time on a combat air patrol, would have insufficient fuel for a prolonged engagement.

Should fighters be detected late in the attack and the range be assessed at 1½ miles or less, it had to be assumed that an Atoll launch was imminent. In this situation it was imperative that the Buccaneer be flown in such a manner as to break the IR lock. The best form of defence was to initiate a maximum rate turn towards the fighters whilst remaining at low level. The navigator's role was to watch the fighters and inform his pilot if missiles were seen to be launched. At this stage in the combat there was nothing to lose, and probably a lot to be gained, by throttling back and extending the airbrakes in order to decelerate violently and reduce the IR emission. Both of these actions would reduce the chances of the missiles holding their lock. In suitable conditions cloud could also be used to break the lock and defeat a missile in flight, and a pull up towards the sun might also have a similar effect, but this was considered to be something of a last resort. Once the missiles were seen to have missed, it was vital that speed be regained as quickly as possible and a careful watch kept for any re-attack by either missiles or guns (in certain cases it might have been possible to release a parachute-retarded 1,000 lb bomb to deter a close-in guns attack. This so-called retard defence was initially referred to as 'dropping your knickers', but after acronyms took over the world it became known as a BIF, which stood for 'Bomb in Face').

In addition to fighters, any low flying Buccaneer would also have had to contend with a range of surface-to-air missiles. In the early 1970s these defences consisted mainly of the semi-mobile S and C-band SA-2 Guideline and the SA-3 Goa, together with the more advanced and fully mobile SA-4 Ganef. These missiles were about to be joined by the formidable SA-6 Gainful which was also fully mobile, but at the time of the CTTO report this SAM system had not entered service. The SA-2 and SA-4 systems were both used as field army weapons and could be expected wherever large infantry or armoured formations were concentrated. This would probably be in the forward battle area and along reasonably well-defined access routes for SA-4 and around large headquarters and storage areas for SA-2. The C-band SA-2 was also used for area defence throughout East Germany. SA-3 missiles were used mainly for airfield defence so as far as penetration was concerned, assuming these sites were known, they could be avoided quite easily.

The threat posed by surface-to-air missiles was virtually the opposite of that from fighters. In visual conditions no penetrating aircraft should ever have been in a position for a successful SAM engagement. This was due to the fact that the normal visual penetration height of 250 ft was well below the lower engagement envelopes of all Soviet missile systems, even the new SA-6. When operating in IMC, however, the Buccaneer generally flew at an altitude of between 500 and 1,000 ft AGL which placed it in danger from all of the deployed SAM systems except the S-band SA-2 which had a lower altitude limit of 1,500 ft. The SA-4 was capable of intercepting a target down to 1,000 ft, the C-band SA-2 was effective down to 750 ft and the SA-3 could operate to a minimum of 500 ft. It was expected that this would also be the limiting height of SA-6. Even though it was theoretically possible to intercept penetrating aircraft, the time available to do so was severely limited and so from the Buccaneer's point of view, speed and height were the most important factors when considering the best tactics to avoid missile engagements.

At the time of the CTTO report not all of the Buccaneer fleet had been fitted with PWR equipment. For aircraft yet to be modified the only defence was to try to fly below the minimum engagement altitudes of the SAM systems. In broad terms this meant keeping below 750 ft to prevent detection by C-band SA-2. In the case of SA-3, penetrating aircraft would either have to keep at least 9 miles away from missile sites at heights above 500 ft or attempt to stay below 500 ft when in the engagement zone. The future deployment of SA-6 would change the threat level yet again as widespread use in the Central Region would mean that flight in this area in IMC would be hazardous at heights above 500 ft.

When PWR equipment was fitted, aircraft penetrating in instrument conditions had a warning period of 30-60 seconds between SAM radar illumination and missile firing. This short period therefore could be used to make the engagement as difficult as possible for the SAM battery. In the event of a confirmed missile threat on the PWR display it was best to reduce height (if possible), turn away from the source of the emission and accelerate. If these actions were taken quickly enough the chances of a missile hit were significantly reduced. Although the Buccaneer stood a good chance of evading Soviet missile defences in the early 1970s thanks to its ability to fly fast and low, the ever improving capability of SAM systems meant that in the future the viability of IMC penetrations would be more and more dependent on responsive active ECM.

The final element in the Soviet defence system was anti-aircraft artillery (AAA) which in the Buccaneer's area of operation was likely to be formidable. However, as far as penetrating aircraft were concerned the picture was not quite as gloomy as it, at first, appeared to be. All of the AAA weapons in the area were used either for the defence of mobile troops or fixed targets, there being no AAA area defence anywhere within the Central Region. As with the SAM threat, instrument and visual conditions presented entirely different problems for both penetrating aircraft and the defending guns. In visual conditions, at the usual penetrating heights flown by the Buccaneer, the opportunity for engagement by guns was small and those guns which did engage would generally only have time for optical tracking and prediction.

In instrument conditions the types of guns capable of engaging an aircraft of the Buccaneer's capability was limited to the 23 mm four-barrel ZSU-23-4 and the 57 mm two-barrel ZSU-57-2. An assessment was made on the effectiveness of these guns against a low flying target, the resultant graphs showing the relationship between speed, height and mean kill probability for visual penetrations below 300 ft and for instrument penetrations at heights of between 500 and 1,000 ft. In visual conditions the best defence for a Buccaneer was to fly as low as possible and if height could be maintained at about 100 ft, there was a wide speed band within which the probability of a kill by gunfire was very low. As height was increased, however, a comparatively large increase in speed was needed to maintain the same vulnerability figure. In instrument conditions between 500 and 1,000 ft, speed was the deciding factor. When up against the ZSU-23-4, for example, at a height of 750 ft an increase in speed from 420 knots to 550 knots reduced the kill probability from approximately 20 per cent down to about 8 per cent.

In assessing the AAA threat to a penetrating aircraft it had to be assumed that it could be engaged by any of the AAA weapons at any stage, and in visual conditions this included chance firings of small calibre weapons as well as the larger 30, 37 and 57 mm guns. The most effective defensive measure was to remain as low as possible and to fly as fast as possible, commensurate with the weapon load and fuel that was being carried. If aircraft were forced to fly at heights above 100 ft speed became increasingly important and transit speeds had to be high at all times. It was also important that the aircraft did not remain in steady flight conditions for too long, a requirement that was particularly relevant when operating in IMC. In these conditions, jinking, consisting of continuous and random height and heading changes, had to be employed. This was particularly important for aircraft without PWR or active ECM equipment. The introduction of passive warning radar gave penetrating aircraft around 15-22 seconds warning of an impending AAA engagement. Provided that the aircraft was jinked immediately and if possible turned away from the threat, the chances of it being hit were significantly reduced. The chances of successfully evading AAA would have been increased still further by the use of ECM to disrupt the gun-laying radars and stop them from achieving a lock-on.

In general it was concluded that the Buccaneer possessed the capability for low-level visual penetrations of Warsaw Pact territory in the Central Region given the level of the Soviet fighter, SAM and AAA defences in the early 1970s. Although transit to and from targets would be carried out at 250 ft or below, it was stressed that significant advantages were to be gained by remaining at heights of 100 ft or even lower. This would obviously place a great burden on operational training and it was recommended that overland visual navigation be made at heights down to 100 ft at representative penetrations speeds, with short periods at speeds of up to 540 knots. Low level handling at high speeds also had to be regularly practiced, including fighter evasion and jinking. It was also important for navigators to recognise and react to the audio warning of Soviet SAM and AAA fire control radars. The increasingly severe restrictions on low-level flying in Western Europe, however, meant that this type of training had to be carried out elsewhere over sparsely populated territory. For Buccaneer crews, the opportunities provided by the Red Flag exercises conducted out of Nellis AFB, together with Maple Flag held over the Cold Lake Air Weapons Range in Canada, gave them realistic training in the type of flying that would be essential if they were to stand a reasonable chance of surviving in a real war situation over northern Europe.

Accidents and Incidents

The Buccaneer suffered its fair share of accidents and incidents during its 33 years in service, a situation that was not particularly surprising considering its complexity and the fact that it had been designed to operate at sea and at ultra low level, the harshest of environments. This chapter looks at some of the mishaps that occurred throughout the aircraft's life to highlight typical situations that its crews were faced with.

LOW SPEED HANDLING

With its dependence on boundary layer control for lift at the low end of the speed range and its T-tail configuration, the Buccaneer had to be watched very carefully as speed was reduced towards the stall. The very first aircraft to be lost was XK490, the fifth prototype NA.39 which crashed near Lyndhurst in Hampshire on 12 October 1959 killing pilot Bill Alford and his observer John Joyce of Blackburn Aircraft. Alford was a civilian employed by NASA and was based at Langley Field, Virginia as an Aeronautical Research Engineer and Test Pilot, his role on this occasion being to evaluate the NA.39 for the US Government as the project had been part funded under the Mutual Weapons Development Programme (MWDP). Joyce was an experienced observer who had been with Blackburn since 1953 and had been flying in the NA.39 for 14 months. Several witnesses saw the aircraft dive steeply into the ground in an inverted attitude having descended from an estimated 13,000 ft in a series of 'spins' or 'rolls'. The impact resulted in a crater 20 ft deep and 35 ft across. Both crew members ejected shortly before the aircraft hit the ground but both seats were fired well outside their operating limits. The transcript of R/T communications, together with information from the data monitor retrieved from the crash site, allowed the final moments of the flight to be pieced together.

The aircraft had taken off from Boscombe Down at 1448 hrs and by 1521 hrs was flying at a speed of 150 knots at 12,000 ft for a low speed handling check, probably in the blown configuration with up to 45 degrees of flap, 20 degrees of aileron droop, and 20 degrees of tailplane flap. It continued in this state for a further 6 minutes but shortly afterwards speed was seen to suddenly reduce to around 100 kts IAS and the starboard engine was noted as being at the flight idle position. Wind tunnel tests had shown that the NA.39 would stall in the clean configuration at about 140 kts IAS but that with full blow and drooped aileron, stall speed could be reduced to approximately 105 kts IAS. With one engine at full rpm the stall speed would be about 112 kts IAS but with both engines at idle, stall speed would be considerably higher at 120-130 kts IAS. In the latter case with drooped ailerons but no BLC, any asymmetry was likely to produce a fairly abrupt wing-tip stall.

Within a few seconds the aircraft was down to 10,000 ft and was sinking rapidly and the data showed that both engines were at flight idle (approximately 5,000 rpm). It was at this point that the data appeared to show a pitch down, but opinion was divided as to whether this was caused by a natural downwards pitch in the stalled state, or was the result of deliberate recovery action with the tailplane. Speed increased for a short time and the aircraft probably unstalled itself during this period, but soon after it was noted as being at 10,500 ft, the increase in height indicating a significant pitch up into the fully stalled state from the unstalled condition. This led to the speed dropping to 70 kts IAS and a resumption of the descent, this time at a vastly increased rate of around 250 ft/sec or 15,000 ft/min. The aircraft would have been out of control at this point and probably at a high angle of incidence. It is also likely that it would have entered a spin, particularly if there was any asymmetry in the flight conditions. Impact with the ground occurred only 53 seconds after the aircraft's speed had fallen to 100 kts IAS.

At the time of the accident full stalling tests had not been carried out and safeguards for these trials would have included entry to the stall being made at a much greater height (around 25,000 ft) and the use of an anti-spin parachute. Although the data showed that the aircraft was teetering on the edge of a stall for some time, it appears that a critical point in the flight was the throttling back of the second engine which would have resulted in a sharp increase in the stalling speed, leading to a sudden stall. Based on evidence from the crash site, the aircraft hit the ground in the clean configuration, so it appears that Alford spent much of the descent cleaning up his aircraft as this would have given a better chance of recovery. It would have been vitally important to get the tailplane flap lowered as quickly as possible, as unless this was done, the aircraft would probably have stayed in a spin. The crew's late ejection also suggests that the pilot thought he could regain control. No pre-crash defects or mechanical failures were found.

Another stall/spin accident occurred on 18 August 1962 at Lossiemouth and involved XK535 of 700Z Flight. The aircraft was being flown by Lieutenant W.W. Foote USN with Lieutenant M.J. Day RN as observer and involved a rehearsal for a forthcoming display at the Farnborough Air Show. The routine comprised a number of runs across the airfield culminating in a fast run at 540 knots at 1,000 ft AGL leading to a LABS manoeuvre. This was to be followed by a roll off the top, a turn to starboard and a descent at 300 knots with full airbrake and 85 per cent rpm. After a descending turn to port onto the runway heading a simulated blown landing was to be made, again at 1,000 ft AGL. This sequence was flown twice during the sortie, the first being completed successfully, although the aircraft was high and fast at the simulated landing threshold.

On the second attempt all went well until the point of the final turn for landing which was made some 3-4,000 ft higher than it should have been. During the turn, or immediately afterwards, the aircraft went into a steep descent until, at a height estimated by witnesses as 5,000 ft, a recovery appeared to be initiated. The aircraft was seen to spin two or three times to starboard, check, and then spin to port. This spin was again checked and an attempt was made to recover, but by this time the descent angle was extremely steep and the aircraft crashed into the sea approximately 2 miles off Lossiemouth harbour. The pilot ejected at around 200 ft but although his parachute was seen to stream it did not fill. The observer ejected later still and neither crewmen survived.

One interesting aspect of this accident was that the leading edge BLC had been made inoperative and pilots had been instructed to add 5 knots to the datum speed. With leading edge BLC disconnected, the blowing system magnetic indicator would also have been inoperative so that blow failure would not have been directly indicated to the pilot. Any failure of trailing edge blow would only have been shown on the relevant pressure gauges to the rear of the port console but the positioning of these meant that they were very difficult to read.

Once the aircraft had been salvaged particular attention was given to the ADD unit and the Air Data Computer which showed that the Buccaneer had hit the sea at a speed of 188 knots and an angle of 54 degrees. At the point of impact the undercarriage was down and the main flaps, aileron droop and tailplane flap angles were 45/15/15. As the pilot was due to make a blown landing in the 45/25/25 configuration two possibilities existed. Either the 45/25/25 configuration had been achieved and an attempt was being made to decrease the angles of aileron droop and tailplane flap to aid recovery, or the full landing configuration had been selected but had not yet been fully achieved.

The Board of Inquiry into the accident established that the aircraft was in the blown landing configuration prior to its steep descent and since full flap was not to be selected above 160 knots on the Buccaneer, the speed at this time was probably at or below this figure. It was considered that there were two possibilities as regards the steep descent, either that the pilot was diving to lose height, or that he was diving in an attempt to regain control, this situation having been brought about by aircraft unserviceability. Of the two the latter was thought to be the most likely as it was considered to be extremely improbable that a spin would result from descending flight Assuming that the aircraft had suffered a technical defect, there were a number of possibilities, the most likely being a flying control restriction, engine failure, ADD malfunction, a malfunction of the tailplane flap or runaway trim, or a failure of the blowing system resulting in asymmetric blow. Of these, the latter was the only possibility to be positively supported by evidence.

An examination of the remains of the aircraft showed that the port wing trailing edge blow pressure gauge was reading 0 lb/sq.in at the point of impact, whereas the equivalent starboard gauge was reading 45 lb/sq.in, the pressure which was to be expected in the trailing edge blow duct. This was strong evidence of asymmetric blow which would have resulted in the port wing dropping. In response the pilot would probably have pushed the nose down to increase speed, at the same time as feeding in right rudder to raise the wing. If the pilot had recognised that the aircraft was in asymmetric blow he may well have selected an unblown configuration (45/10/10). This could be an explanation for the 15 degree angles noted for aileron droop and tailplane flap at impact, as the settings may well have been in the process of changing from the 45/25/25 blown configuration to the 45/10/10 unblown condition.

There was further evidence to support the asymmetric blow theory as the port wing trailing edge blow shut off valve was disconnected. This could have occurred on impact but in view of the zero reading of its associated gauge it was felt that this could not be dismissed as pure coincidence. In conclusion, the Board of Inquiry considered the probable cause of the accident to be a loss of blow on the port side at a critical stage in the approach, which led to loss of control from which there was insufficient height to recover. A further factor to be considered was the inoperative blowing system magnetic indicator which may have resulted in the pilot recognising the fault too late, indeed the wisdom of flying the aircraft with the blowing system indicator inoperative was called into question.

Another development batch aircraft was lost on 13 May 1965 when XK524 dived into the ground near Holme-on-Spalding Moor. On this occasion a level acceleration was being made from low speed when the aircraft developed a nose-down pitch which could not be recovered with back stick. As height was less than 2,000 ft the crew, comprising test pilot Paul Millett and observer J. Harris, made a quick exit and both survived. The following is taken from Millett's flight report:

Introduction – A flight was made on 13 May 1965 to gather further data on the 35 degree aileron droop configuration. Control was lost during an attempted level acceleration, the crew both ejecting successfully, the aircraft crashing into a field.

Aircraft Loadings – AUW 39,517 lb, Fuel 12,270 lb, CG 31.42 per cent SMC undercarriage down.

Configuration – The aircraft was fitted with extended chord flaps and ailerons and 35 degrees of aileron droop was available.

Pilot's Clothing – The pilot was wearing a lightweight flying suit, Mk.1 protection and inner helmet and flying boots.

Ejection Seats – The aircraft was fitted with Mk.4MS1 ejection seats.

Flight Details – The take-off was made in the blown 30/30/25 configuration with the tailplane trimmed at -5½ degrees and -11 degrees held on the stick. The nosewheel came off at 123 knots and the aircraft unstuck at 128 knots. The undercarriage only was retracted after take off and this was lowered again shortly afterwards and the airbrakes selected fully out at about 1,000 ft. The intention was to make a level acceleration from 23 units ADD to 150 knots, but continuous light turbulence made accurate flying difficult, so the acceleration was finally made from about 21½ units ADD, 120 kts IAS up to 150 kts IAS. The acceleration was made by selecting full power and airbrakes in simultaneously and attempting to hold level flight. Trim changes were small and normal, the main one being nose up as the speed increased.

A second acceleration was made from about 21½ units ADD, 115 kts IAS in the 45/35/25 configuration at 1,250 ft. Trim changes were similar to the first acceleration. The aircraft was set up for a third acceleration in the following conditions – undercarriage down, configuration 45/35/30, airbrakes out, ADD 19 units, IAS 117 kts, altitude 1,700 ft, power for level flight approximately 93.5 – 94 per cent rpm, continuous light turbulence. After waiting for some time for some relatively smooth air, an acceleration was commenced in the same manner as before, by selecting full power and airbrakes in together. Shortly after starting this acceleration at about 130 knots, the aircraft started a steady nose down pitch. Aft stick movement to counteract this had no apparent effect on the rate of pitch, so the observer was told to eject and the pilot immediately ejected.

Pilot Ejection – The ejection was made through the canopy. The recommended Buccaneer ejection technique is to jettison the canopy before ejection, but this was not considered at the time and in any case the pilot had decided a long time before not to bother to jettison the canopy unless plenty of time was available for a controlled ejection. The primary firing handle was found without difficulty and pulled with both hands. The seat fired almost immediately with a surprising force and an associated sharp pain in the back, and after a sensation of tumbling in the seat, the parachute deployed with a very satisfying strong tug. During the ejection, possibly on pulling the face blind, the protective helmet had slipped forward over the pilot's eyes and after pushing it back into place, the aircraft was seen diving towards the ground and the observer's parachute was seen about 500 ft below and close to the ground.

Some parachute oscillation was taking place but it did not feel excessive so no attempt was made to counteract it, although the hands were put up to the forward lift web and they were gripped in the approved fashion. The landing was made in a pasture field whilst drifting backwards and to the right and a heavy landing was made flat on the back. No difficulty was found in turning and releasing the quick release button after landing.

It was considered that the accident was most probably caused by a stalling, or partial stalling of the tailplane brought about by the trim change resulting from the simultaneous retraction of the airbrakes and the application of full power. A further contributory factor was the light turbulence that was experienced during the flight as this would have led to the pilot having to apply further negative tailplane angle to balance the aircraft at a critical moment.

INSTRUMENT FAILURE

The prototype NA.39 (XK486) crashed in unfortunate circumstances on 5 October 1960 when engaged on autopilot trials. It was being flown near Holme-on-Spalding Moor by Blackburn test pilot G.R.I 'Sailor' Parker, with E.J.D. Nightingale as observer, when control was lost in cloud as a result of a defective Artificial Horizon Indicator which was giving a false reading. As Parker had already had two dicey moments with the NA.39 (a tailplane control restriction in XK489 and a similar problem affecting the aileron on XK486), he wasted no time in ordering his observer to bale out, before doing the same himself. The following is Dave Nightingale's view of what happened,

We completed a dive from Mach 0.80 to 0.96 coming down from 20,000 ft and recovering at 14,000 ft. We then overflew Holme-on-Spalding Moor and the autopilot was engaged for a check. It seemed fairly reasonable but the weather was very bad. Prior to doing the run we heard that there was an aircraft in our vicinity coming from Brough and so we went off on a northerly heading. We were still trying to find a clear lane for a level run when Sailor said "Not to worry, the weather is too bad, we can't do it at this height". He then asked Holme for a radar climb

We started to climb (I was writing notes at the time) and then I felt that the aircraft was adopting a rather peculiar attitude – I found out afterwards that we were yawing. I then heard Sailor say 'Bale out, bale out, bale out' and the canopy was blown. The wind tore at my flying overalls and then I found that my right arm was above my head. I found it impossible to pull my right arm down with my left hand so I attempted to grab hold of the pan handle. I eventually managed to get hold of it, pulled it and felt myself going out. I don't remember being separated from my seat.

We were still in cloud when my parachute deployed. I remember thinking at the time 'What a bloody small parachute this is!' I felt behind and there was no seat and I just drifted down. I came down through two cloud levels, it was snowing in one and raining in t'other! After breaking through the cloud I found that I was drifting towards a large pond so I spilt some air from the parachute and fairly rapidly moved away from it. Unfortunately I was then confronted with a wood, a road and some telegraph wires. I happened to go through the biggest blasted tree in the wood and eventually became entangled with my leg restraining strap on an iron railing. I had to cut my rigging with the help of a farmer who came along and then extricated myself. I suffered bruises but that was all. It was a very clean separation, there was no pain but it was very frightening.

Nightingale had only recently joined the Blackburn company and this flight was only his second in an NA.39. It was later calculated that Parker had ejected at 400 knots but that Nightingale had got out some time later by which time the aircraft had slowed to around 250 knots. The fact that he had suffered no injuries, apart from minor bruising, was put down to careful and meticulous strapping in during the pre-flight routine. Nightingale's ejection was also the first successful ejection in the UK using the secondary pan firing handle instead of the primary face-blind handle.

TAKE-OFF ACCIDENTS

The first aircraft to be lost at sea was NA.39 XK529 which crashed shortly after being launched from the aircraft carrier HMS *Hermes* on 31 August 1961 during a series of deck trials. At the time XK529 was being flown by Lieutenant-Commander 'Ossie' Brown RN with Trevor Dunn of Blackburn Aircraft in the rear seat. It was launched from the port catapult at an all-up weight of 37,926 lb, but after leaving the deck the aircraft developed a nose-high attitude which progressively increased until it stalled and plunged into the sea approximately 500 yards ahead of the ship. The time from launch to impact was 11 seconds and although the aircraft floated for a further 27 seconds before sinking, neither of the crew were able evacuate it before it went down.

At the time of leaving the catapult, aircraft incidence was 11½ degrees with a pitch rate of 2 degrees per second (the tailplane having been set to -13 degrees). At slightly less than half a second after launch the pitch rate had grown to 5 degrees per second and at this point the tailplane moment suddenly reversed to a nose down position achieving a rate of 20 degrees per second. In achieving this corrective action in the shortest possible time, the pilot applied a stick force considerably greater than that required to hold full forward deflection. Two seconds after launch the pitch rate was still 5 degrees per second (having come down from a maximum of 11 degrees per second) but aircraft incidence was now 21½ degrees. At this moment the rate of pitch-up changed again indicating that something had occurred to outweigh the corrective action of the tailplane. This was most likely to have been the stalling of the wing tips which would have resulted in a forwards movement of the Centre of Pressure.

The obvious solution to the accident was that the aircraft had simply been over-rotated. During previous deck trials there had been occasional nose-down pitches after launch to the point where the aircraft had descended below deck level and this may have led the pilot to over-correct in anticipation of this occurrence happening again. There was, however, some evidence of a reduction in blow which would have had the effect of causing the wing to stall earlier, thus causing a nose-up pitch. Defects were noted in the latch pin joints of the wing fold system. The port front latch pin was missing and was not recovered and the rear latch pin was well short of full engagement. It had been demonstrated that wing deflection, if of sufficient magnitude, could reduce the BLC system pressure to a critical value. There was a possibility, therefore, that port-wing deflection during the launch had affected the blowing system and this may have been a contributory factor in the accident. If so it would have materially altered the performance characteristics of the aircraft to an extent that, unbeknown to the pilot, rendered a previously satisfactory take off technique unsafe.

The RAF had their fair share of take-off mishaps with the Buccaneer but by the very nature of their operations there was usually more time available to save the situation. On 12 May 1971 XV351 of 12 Squadron was taking off from the Danish airfield of Karup as the No.2 of a pair in echelon port with power set at 93 per cent rpm, when the starboard tyre burst at around 160 knots. The nosewheel was still on the ground and the aircraft lurched to starboard, the pilot immediately electing to abandon the take-off and lower the hook (the stop speed for 100 per cent rpm had previously been calculated at 149 knots). The runway that was being used (09) had two barriers, the main one was down with the lower wire forming a hookwire and a secondary Safeland barrier was in the overrun area, approximately 195 yards after the main barrier, to protect a boundary road. Unfortunately this was incapable of being lowered and was to cause something of a problem as the Buccaneer was not cleared for barrier entry as it was fitted with an AAR probe.

The pilot was unaware that the second barrier could not be lowered and some time was lost as he called for it to be taken down. In his preoccupation with this, he omitted to use the airbrakes or the nosewheel steering during the ensuing period of heavy braking. He did not shut down the engines as he needed hydraulic pressure for the brakes and he also decided not to jettison the wing tanks as he considered that they might catch fire and follow the aircraft into the barrier. The navigator was concerned that the top wire of the Safeland barrier might bite down into his cockpit and so he ejected shortly before the aircraft entered the barrier complex. Although he landed safely, he sustained a back injury which required a lengthy period off duty. The Buccaneer took the main barrier hookwire at a speed of 110 knots in the centre of the runway and finally came to rest in soft sandy soil after also engaging the second barrier. The pilot did not eject and was uninjured. Some damage was caused to the aircraft during the barrier entry but temporary repairs allowed it to be flown back to base (wheels down) nine days later.

CONTROL PROBLEMS

Like most other complex aircraft the Buccaneer occasionally suffered from control problems in which there was a sudden change in the aircraft's attitude without any input from the pilot through the controls. Such an event occurred on 17 June 1982 and resulted in the total loss of a Buccaneer S.2B of 12 Squadron. On returning to Lossiemouth having carried out a night sortie, the crew of XX898 were on short finals to land at a height of 550 feet when the aircraft yawed sharply to the left. The pilot immediately attempted to counteract the yaw by applying right rudder but this was ineffective and the yaw was soon accompanied by roll in the same direction. As the nose also began to drop it was clear that the situation was irrecoverable and both crew members ejected successfully, although both received serious back injuries in the process. The Buccaneer continued its descending turn to crash in a field 1½ miles south-west of Lossiemouth.

The inquiry into the accident discovered that the control rod to the rudder was not connected to the Power Control Unit (PCU) and although the relevant connecting bolt was found in the wreckage, there was no sign of the nut and split pin. This discovery led the investigators to examine the aircraft's service history and it was found that the last major service had occurred eight months previously during which the rudder PCU had been replaced. Since then XX898 had flown a total of 148 hours. It was assumed that during the service the split pin had not been fitted and in the intervening period the nut had gradually worked loose to the point where it had broken away from the bolt and had allowed the control rod to disconnect from the PCU. To test the validity of this assumption, experiments were carried out on a Buccaneer rudder PCU to see what would happen if the control rod became detached. It was discovered that the PCU would immediately apply full left rudder irrespective of the control surface deflection prior to the disconnection.

Another incident in the early 1980s showed a rather different control problem. A Buccaneer was taking off as the No.2 in a four-aircraft section, but as the pilot eased the control column back at 160 knots to raise the nose a significant overrotation was experienced which needed almost full forward stick to counteract. This sensitivity in pitch was most alarming and occurred despite the fact that the aircraft was being operated at a high all-up weight. The settings for flaps and aileron droop were maintained up to a height of 4,000 ft and during the climb it was established that there was only ½ inch of forward stick movement available. Even with this stick position the tailplane indicator was showing a reading of four degrees nose up. Despite jettisoning fuel to lower weight, the pilot was of the opinion that there would still not be enough control authority to make a safe landing and so he discussed the problem with his navigator and the pilot of another Buccaneer. Eventually it was decided that the best course of action would be to operate the emergency flap and droop selectors which would have the effect of producing a nose-down pitch that was likely to increase the extremely limited tailplane authority. A low speed handling check at a safe height showed there was now approximately 1½ inches of forward stick available and having burned off more fuel, the aircraft was able to land without mishap.

Control problems could be encountered at any time and the outcome was often dependent on the aircraft's altitude and also its attitude when the difficulties were encountered. On 9 February 1972 Buccaneer S.2 XN974 was taking part in an exercise which involved a vari-toss manoeuvre. The pilot initiated the manoeuvre at a height of 300 ft ASL and a speed of 560 knots.

Four seconds after the pull up, the pitch rate of the aircraft reduced noticeably and was accompanied by a marked increase in the tailplane control stick forces. The aircraft then suddenly pitched nose down and entered a violent short period oscillation. It was later ascertained from the trace recordings that loadings of +7g to -3g were experienced for a period of 1½ to 2 seconds. The pilot exerted a steady backward pull on the control column and was careful not to chase the movement which would only have served to make the oscillation worse. No damping was apparent at this time or even when the pilot released the controls for a brief period. Only when the auto-stabilisers were isolated did the oscillations damp out to half amplitude and eventually they disappeared altogether.

As far as the crew were concerned it was fortunate that this particular incident occurred when the aircraft was climbing, if it had taken place a few seconds before they would have been in great danger. The pilot was commended for his actions, particularly as it would have been easy to induce increased oscillations by attempting to oppose the cyclical motion that the aircraft had adopted. An investigation subsequently revealed a defective Pitch Rate Gyro and a faulty Power Supply Module in the autopilot computer. To be on the safe side the complete computer was returned to the manufacturers for testing (XN974 was the first production S.2 and is kept in ground running condition at the Yorkshire Air Museum at Elvington near York).

ENGINE FAILURES
As already recounted in Chapter Eight, the Buccaneer S.2 suffered from serious engine problems in its early service life, and the following examples illustrate some of the failures that were experienced. On 9 December 1971, having carried out the pre-flight checks without incident, the crew of XV347 of 12 Squadron began their take-off roll. While the engines were still accelerating, however, a loud bang was heard. The aircraft was quickly brought to a halt but it was immediately apparent that the port engine was on fire. As the pilot and navigator vacated the Buccaneer from the starboard side, the emergency crews sprang into action but they were not able to prevent the fuselage and the port wing from burning out completely. Despite the level of damage it was found that the port engine had suffered a circumferential fracture of the low pressure compressor drum to the rear of the 3rd stage and forward of the attachment flange to the compressor shaft extension. The top half of the low pressure compressor casing had been blown off and a blade from either stage 2 or 3 had penetrated a fuel tank, causing the fire.

On another occasion a Buccaneer was in the pattern at the Nordhorn bombing range in Germany when the crew members felt a sudden vibration which appeared to emanate from the centre section. The sortie was quickly aborted but soon after a loud bang was heard and there was a loss of power from the port engine. The nearest diversion airfield was the German Air Force base at Hopsten but the transit there was complicated by the illumination of several warning captions on the cockpit displays. The first to show was the port-engine fire warning which remained on for around 30 seconds despite the pilot carrying out a full fire-drill. It then went out which encouraged the crew to stay with the aircraft but shortly after it was followed by a port flying-controls pressure warning and failure of the master fuel-gauges. On final approach into Hopsten the navigator saw black smoke coming from the port engine but the aircraft landed without further trouble and the situation was then taken over by the fire crews who were ready and waiting.

The subsequent investigation established a sequence of events, the first of which was an HP (high-pressure) turbine failure. This would have accounted for the initial vibration that the crew had felt and this was most likely followed by the rupture of an LP (low-pressure) fuel-filter pipe connection. This would have led to fuel coming into contact with the engine which would have started a fire. The turbine then seized which led to the loss of power from the port engine. As the fire spread further, damage was also caused to electrical wiring, control rods and the airframe itself with considerable buckling being apparent in the vicinity of the No.2 fuel tank. The damage was later assessed as Cat 3 and took around 8,000 man hours to put right.

A similar sequence of events led to the loss of Buccaneer S.2B XW548 of 16 Squadron on 3 February 1977. The Laarbruch-based aircraft caught fire in the air during a training sortie and crashed near the military airfield of Volkel in the Netherlands. On this occasion both crew members ejected safely. The members of the Board of Inquiry that was set up to investigate the cause of the crash were not unduly troubled during their investigations, as it was immediately obvious that there had been an uncontained turbine failure in the starboard engine. This was evident on examination of the wreckage as jagged holes were noted in the turbine casing caused by the disintegrating turbine blades. This process had also led to significant damage to the airframe in the immediate area of the starboard engine and a fire in the engine bay. Given the catastrophic nature of the engine disintegration, only the quick reactions of the crew prevented there being a double fatality.

LOW LEVEL OPERATIONS

As the Buccaneer spent much of its life operating at low level the inherent dangers as a result of birdstrikes flying in close proximity to sea or land and collision with other aircraft were high on the list of hazards faced by aircrews. Two examples from 1972 serve to illustrate the problem of birdstrikes. On 5 April XW530 was in the final stages of a simulated laydown bombing attack when two buzzards were seen to pass either side of the aircraft. No impact was felt, although this may have been due to conditions of moderate turbulence that were being experienced at the time. On landing it was clear that the aircraft had been hit as the port-wing inboard leading-edge section and its corresponding internal structure had been damaged sufficiently to warrant a Cat 3 repair. A more serious birdstrike occurred on 9 June when XV332 was on the run in for an attack on a bombing range at 400 ft and 550 knots. A large flock of gulls was seen too late to take avoiding action and the aircraft received multiple hits which shattered the pilot's canopy. After a low speed handling check and an inspection by another aircraft, a safe landing was made. In addition to the damage caused to the canopy, the outer skin of the radome was partly torn off, the starboard intake and engine were damaged by debris, the UHF aerial was cracked and the tailplane bullet fairing was punctured.

As the Buccaneer's role dictated that it was to fly at ultra low level for prolonged periods, this brought with it the very real possibility of flying into the ground/sea, especially at night. On 4 January 1972 the crews of two Buccaneers were briefed for a night ground-attack mission on the range at Jurby on the Isle of Man. Although the lead crew were experienced on the Buccaneer, the pilot of the second aircraft (Squadron Leader T.G. 'Jock' Gilroy) was relatively inexperienced on type having accumulated a total of 80 hours, of which 25 hours were in the previous month. His navigator was Flight Lieutenant C. Willbourne who had spent much of his career on PR Canberras and had recently completed the Buccaneer OCU course. The transit from Honington to Jurby was uneventful but on joining the range, an unserviceability on the No.2 aircraft led to this part of the mission being aborted. The leader of the formation advised his No.2 to rejoin formation and advised him that they would carry out an alternative low-level exercise to the south. Squadron Leader Gilroy called that he was in visual contact with the lead aircraft as it was passing over the target and the No.1 then transmitted on the squadron discreet radio frequency, but had to call three times before receiving a reply. Gilroy was then ordered into night formation, which he acknowledged, giving his position at the time as 1,000 yards range in the lead aircraft's 5 o'clock position. Although the formation leader kept a good lookout during a slow descent to 600 ft ASL, he was unable to see the other aircraft and it did not respond to repeated radio calls.

At around this time a number of civilians on the southern half of the western coast of the Isle of Man were startled by a bright flash which lit up the western sky. This was followed by a red and orange fireball on the surface of the sea followed by a rising pall of black smoke. The position and timing of the explosion coincided with the time that the lead aircraft would have been passing. The subsequent Board of Inquiry had little to work on and although a technical defect could not be ruled out, there was no direct evidence of this. The body of Flight Lieutenant Willbourne was trawled up by a fishing boat near to the position of the crash and that of Squadron Leader Gilroy was recovered later.

Another hazard of low-level operations was the risk of collision and this led to the loss of XW535 of 16 Squadron on 24 January 1973. A new squadron pilot was to fly a FAM 2 sortie with an experienced navigator, comprising a low level navex at 1,000 ft followed by a descent to 500 ft after 30 minutes and a practice diversion. The sortie was uneventful until near a turning point when, with the aircraft flying at 800 ft AGL and 420 kts IAS, the pilot entered a left-hand turn which was stabilised with about 60 degrees of bank. This manoeuvre was seen by another Buccaneer which was following the same route and was about 2,000 yards behind. At some point in this turn the pilot of XW535 saw the other aircraft and initiated a violent evasive manoeuvre during which both he and his navigator ejected. They landed safely with only minor injuries.

The Board of Inquiry that took place to investigate the crash held that the pilot of XW535, on seeing the other Buccaneer, assessed it to be closing on him and that there was a potential risk that the two aircraft would collide. He thus pulled back hard on the stick whilst in the turn, but this caused a pitch up that was severe enough to stall the aircraft. It was also suggested that he was slow to recognise the stall which meant that recovery action was delayed. In mitigation it was stated that the pilot had completed the OCU course some seven months before and since then had only flown eight Buccaneer sorties on short refresher courses. This accident led to a review of aircrew competency and a reassessment of such a delayed movement to an operational squadron.

AIR-TO-AIR REFUELLING
Always a tricky aspect of fast jet flying, air-to-air refuelling operations produced some moments of drama for Buccaneer crews including the total loss of one aircraft. This was S.2 XV978 which was to have taken part in the Paris Air Show on 5 June 1971 as part of a refuelling demonstration with a Victor tanker. Although turbulence at low level was not excessive, there was variable visibility and occasionally the aircraft flew into cloud. Following several unsuccessful attempts to engage the basket, the Buccaneer pilot had one last go at a height of 3,000 ft but only managed to set up a pilot induced oscillation which culminated in a situation where, during an upward oscillation, the ADD warning went to the low (stall warning) note. The pilot felt that he was beginning to lose control and being aware of the proximity of the ground he ordered the navigator to eject and followed himself shortly after.

Both crew members survived but received major back injuries.

Two weeks later on 18 June 1971 the crew of another Buccaneer (XV353) had to come to terms with a rather different problem. The aircraft was one of a pair of Buccaneers to be refuelled by a Victor tanker. After taking on fuel from the port underwing pod, a withdrawal was initiated but instead of the receiver separating from the tanker, the hose was pulled completely from the pod. The hose remained attached to the Buccaneer and flailed across the canopy and spine of the aircraft as far as the starboard rear fuselage, underneath the fin. An emergency diversion was made into Lossiemouth and the aircraft landed successfully after a straight-in approach with the hose still attached. An inspection showed much damage to paintwork, a punctured rudder and damaged VHF and UHF aerials.

An investigation into this incident showed the Mk.20B pod equipment to have been fully serviceable during the refuelling operation and the most likely cause was a rapid hose withdrawal, one that was too fast for the trail brake to engage. Although the brake tried to operate it was probably damaged in the process and with no brake, the hose ran out to the full trail stop which, in turn, sheared, as it tried to engage the fast moving hose. The hose was then free to run right out and fracture when the full load was taken by the damaged end. The final safety link in the chain, the 'weak link' shear rivets in the Buccaneer probe, did not break. It was considered that the rivets would only shear in a straight pull off, but in the circumstances of this incident the hose proved to be weaker than the rivets. This was the second time that a refuelling hose had broken off from the tanker when a Buccaneer was attempting to disengage which suggested that the Buccaneer probe was somewhat over-engineered!

FATIGUE CRACKS

Although the Buccaneer had a reputation for being one of the toughest of military aircraft, the punishment that it received in its low altitude role led to severe fatigue problems. Cracks had already been discovered in relatively low time aircraft in the early 1970s (see Chapter Eight) but rather more serious fatigue became apparent a few years later. On 12 July 1979 a Buccaneer from 16 Squadron (XW526) crashed near Osnabruck after a structural failure of the starboard wing. Its crew members, Flight Lieutenant A. Colvin and Squadron Leader D. Coupland, were both killed. The Buccaneer fleet was grounded as a result of the accident, however, the cause was quickly shown to be a failure of the forward latch pin on the starboard wing, and as very few other aircraft were affected in this area, the grounding was soon lifted.

Not long after, on 7 February 1980, another Buccaneer (XV345), this time from XV Squadron, crashed whilst taking part in the Red Flag exercises out of Nellis Air Force Base in Nevada. Buccaneers had been among the first RAF aircraft to take part in this realistic 'war game' in 1977 (alongside two Vulcans) and the favourable impression that they made on this first visit led to regular participation. As in the previous case of fatigue the starboard wing broke off under moderate load and the crew consisting of Squadron Leader K.J. Tait and Flight Lieutenant C.R. Ruston were killed. Once again the Buccaneer was grounded as investigations took place to find the cause. The critical area was quickly established as the wing had failed at the root in the vicinity of wing rib 80 and it was found that a serious fatigue crack had developed in the front spar at this point. The tailplane had also departed during the break up but it appeared that this was secondary to the main failure in the wing.

One of the puzzling aspects of this crash was that the structural test airframe at Brough had been tested to six times that of the aircraft with the highest fatigue life and no problems had been experienced. The answer to this paradox was eventually found in the area of the wing tip which had been extended on the S.2 to increase range. This modification had resulted in much more stress being applied to the front spar than had been expected and was responsible for the discrepancy between the test results and the actual fatigue experienced by service aircraft. An examination of the rest of the fleet showed that, in this case, many other aircraft were affected to a greater or lesser degree, the worst having a fatigue crack which was 1.5 inches long (the crack in XV345 had measured 0.6 inch). This was found in XW538 which together with XV340, the aircraft with the highest fatigue life, was tested at Brough to assess structural integrity. Both aircraft were found to be in generally good condition, but problem areas were identified which would need constant monitoring.

After a grounding which had lasted six months, the Buccaneers began to take to the skies once more, however, a number of aircraft with well developed fatigue cracks never flew again. Of the remainder, some had replacement front spars fitted by BAe and the others had the cracks blended out, some aircraft also had the enlarged wing tips removed. Throughout the rest of the Buccaneer's service life, regular airframe inspections prevented the occurrence of any further structural problems.

CHAPTER TWELVE

Pilot Debrief – 1

During a long RAF career, Group Captain Tom Eeles accumulated over 8,000 hours flying time of which nearly 2,200 hours were on the Buccaneer. In this chapter he describes his first involvement with the aircraft which saw him join 801 Squadron of the Fleet Air Arm aboard HMS *Victorious* which was operating in the Far East.

During my first tour, flying Canberras in Germany, I was offered the opportunity of an exchange posting to the Fleet Air Arm, to fly Buccaneers. Being an unattached bachelor I accepted with alacrity, much to the amazement of the rest of my squadron colleagues. After the relative simplicity of the Canberra, the Buccaneer was altogether a much more complex aircraft. Designed originally to deliver a nuclear weapon against Russian capital ships, it was also a very capable conventional attack aircraft and it could deliver a wide range of weapons. It had a well designed cockpit with an excellent view for both crew members. It was designed to fly at high subsonic speeds at very low level, which it did extremely well.

The Buccaneer S.1 was built in relatively small numbers and was being steadily replaced by the S.2, however, the conversion squadron, 736 NAS, was still equipped mainly with S.1s. These were powered by de Havilland Gyron Junior engines which were rather unreliable and short of thrust. Large amounts of air were taken off the engines to provide air for the boundary layer control system which was needed so that the aircraft could fly slowly enough to perform arrested landings on aircraft carriers. Thus take-offs were very slow events and in the approach configuration the aircraft was distinctly underpowered. The S.2 was powered by Rolls-Royce Speys, which had considerably more thrust than the Gyron Junior, and as a consequence it was a much more sprightly performer. The Buccaneer was the first jet aircraft designed exclusively for the Royal Navy from the outset, so it was the star of the Fleet Air Arm.

There were eight of us on our conversion course, two naval pilots (one of whom is now the Airbus chief pilot with Virgin) and two naval observers, the other four were all RAF, two navigators and two pilots. The course itself was very demanding. Initial conversion to the aircraft was a challenge in that there was no dual control version so your first sortie was your first solo, with a QFI in the back seat offering advice on handling, often in no uncertain terms! Once type conversion was complete it was straight into navigation, formation, weapons system handling and weapon delivery sorties on the two local weapons ranges at Tain and Rosehearty. Then we had a busy session of practice deck landings on the runway, known as 'MADDLs' (Mirror Assisted Dummy Deck Landings).

The runway was marked out in the same way as a carrier flight deck with a projector sight alongside, but somehow you could not get the feel of what it really would be like, because whatever you did the runway never moved, it was always 8,000 ft long and 150 ft wide and never pitched up and down. The target area for landing was roughly the size of a tennis court – not very big. You had to be right on the centre line and accurate to within 1 knot of speed, and you had to fly the glide path with total concentration. You made no attempt to flare as you simply flew the aircraft onto the runway. We also went to do Deck Landing Practice (DLP) when a carrier was around.

The first time you see an aircraft carrier from the air your immediate reaction is that it would be quite impossible to land on it, as it was far too small. However, after two sessions of DLP I was declared competent, so there only remained the requirement to experience a catapult shot. There was a shore catapult installation at the research establishment at Bedford and so three of us went down there to do three catapult shots before going to sea. The catapult at Bedford was an amazing device, with a large adjacent boiler house generating the required quantities of steam and looking like a Chinese laundry. You taxied up a ramp on to the catapult itself and were fired off down a disused runway, which had a large barrier like a tennis net to stop you if the catapult did not give you enough flying speed. Because there was no ship generated head wind you always got a very fierce kick from this land-based device. On my final cat shot at Bedford I had a full fuel load for the return to Lossiemouth. The cat gave me such a powerful kick that the entire head-up display became detached and fell on my lap!

The technique used for launching a Buccaneer was 'hands off'. A tailplane trim setting was calculated, taking into account the aircraft's weight, centre of gravity, configuration and expected end speed after launch. This was set and the theory was that it would rotate the aircraft into the correct attitude for the initial climb without intervention from the pilot. Once positioned on the catapult the aircraft would be tensioned up, with its retractable tail skid resting on the deck. The pilot would apply full power and when happy, lock his left arm behind the throttles to ensure they remained at full power, raise his right hand to accept the launch then place it on his right thigh close to, but not holding the control column. The catapult would fire after a short delay.

Acceleration along the deck was phenomenal, 0 to 120 knots in about 1½ seconds, and then everything stopped as you got airborne. It was like being fired into jelly. You then carefully took control by grasping the control column, retracted the landing gear and allowed the aircraft to accelerate to a safe climbing speed, retracting the aileron droop/flap combination in stages. Loss of an engine or boundary layer control air would mean instant ejection. The aircraft was very sensitive in pitch and it was important not to apply a large nose-up control input until a safe speed had been achieved. Cat shots were always exciting and you had no options if something went wrong other than ejection. There was an underwater escape facility fitted to the ejection seat, which, if selected, would release you from the seat and propel you upward if you went into the sea still in the aircraft. However, the canopy had to be jettisoned first and most of us thought that we would come up right under the ship, not a healthy prospect. Few people bothered to select it on.

I was posted to 801 Squadron, HMS *Victorious*, which at that time was in the Far East. Number 801 were the first squadron to be equipped with the Buccaneer S.2 and *Victorious* was halfway through her commission, so I would be joining an experienced outfit. I will never forget my first arrested landing; the deceleration was amazing but even more alarming was the urgency with which you were marshalled away from the angled flight deck to your parking spot, often with only the sea in view. Having finally shut down and climbed out, I looked around. Normally, after landing at an airfield and getting out, all relative motion has ceased and this is what you expect to see. By now though, the ship was turning out of wind; I looked up, expecting the world to be still, but the horizon was moving rapidly. It was so disorientating that I had to clutch hold of the aircraft ladder to stop myself falling over.

Life on board soon settled down as we found our way around and got used to the routine. The flying was probably the most exciting and demanding that I have ever experienced. We started the day early, first launch usually being at 0700 hrs, which meant getting up at 0500 hrs, breakfast in the Aircrew Refreshment Buffet (ACRB) at 0530 hrs – always greasy fried eggs – then briefing at 0600 hrs. The aircraft would be ranged on the flight deck in order of launching – normally the Gannet AEW aircraft first, then the Buccaneers and last of all the Sea Vixens. After start-up the aircraft was taxied forward to the catapult and positioned accurately with the use of the inward rotating rollers that ensured the aircraft was aligned exactly in the centre of the catapult. The hold back, which was a frangible metal link connected to the rear of the aircraft, was then connected to the deck. The aircraft's wings were then spread and the catapult bridle attached; the aircraft was then tensioned on the catapult in the flying attitude. On receipt of the clearance to launch from Flyco, the Flight Deck Officer (FDO) would give the wind-up signal; once the pilot signalled that he was happy to launch, the FDO would drop his green flag and the catapult would fire after a short pause.

Once airborne and joined-up as a formation we would practice a variety of activities. Ship attack profiles, navigation exercises, weapon delivery work, air-to-air-refuelling, battle formation and air combat, strikes on coastal or inland targets all featured regularly. The ship tended to operate either close to Malaya or the Philippines, there being excellent American facilities in the Philippines including the enormous naval support base at Subic Bay. I was lucky enough to be selected not only to deliver a 'Red Beard' 2,000 lb nuclear weapon shape on a 'Long Toss' attack on Tabones Range in the Philippines, but also to fire Bullpup missiles at Scarborough Shoal, an offshore reef with a wreck that made a suitable target. The 'Red Beard' was the British tactical nuclear weapon of that period, designed as the principal anti-ship weapon for the Buccaneer. It filled the entire bomb bay. The target was a small rocky island and the enormous bomb hit it right in the middle – a very satisfying experience.

The Bullpup was a small air-to-surface missile of US origin, with a range of about 3 to 4 miles. It was fired in a shallow dive and controlled by the pilot, using a small control handle. It was a difficult missile to control accurately and much practice was needed on the very simple simulator that we had on board. On one occasion I recovered to the ship after failing to fire a Bullpup due to bad weather. On landing the missile broke free from the aircraft and careered off down the flight deck, narrowly missing various personnel and other aircraft, to fall in the sea ahead of the ship with a big splash. Naturally it was assumed by all that I had failed to make my weapons switches safe and had fired it off by mistake – luckily the film taken from Flyco, when developed, proved otherwise and I was exonerated.

Recovery to the ship was always a fairly stressful business. First of all you had to find the ship which was not always where she said she was. You then joined the 'low wait', to await your 'Charlie time', the time you had to arrive on the deck. When called into 'slot' you joined the circuit, having dumped fuel if necessary to get down to landing weight. The circuit was flown at 600 ft, turning in abeam the ship. You aimed to achieve your final approach speed/angle of attack about half way round the final turn. It was important not to line up on the ship's wake, which always gave a powerful visual distraction, and you also had to cope with the funnel smoke which sometimes was quite thick. The final part of the approach was flown at a constant speed/angle of attack, lined up exactly on the flight deck centre line and using the projector sight for glideslope. It was vital to concentrate utterly on the sight and the centre line, ignoring the rest of the ship's structure. There was no attempt to cushion the landing at all, as a consequence the aircraft arrived at a fairly high rate of descent.

You knew immediately if you had caught a wire because of the very rapid deceleration. In this case you throttled back immediately, so that the aircraft would be pulled back a short distance at the end of its roll out, thereby allowing the wire to fall clear of the arrestor hook. Flight deck handlers would move out onto the flight deck as soon as they saw that you had caught a wire, to give the signals for taxiing clear as quickly as possible, as there was usually another aircraft about 30-40 seconds behind you. The wire needed to be reset and checked before the next aircraft could land – this was done by a man wearing a large glove which he ran down the length of the wire to check for any broken strands. If any were found that wire would not be reset. It was not uncommon for a recovery to start with all four wires available and to finish with only one. You meanwhile taxied clear as fast as possible, folding the wings as you went, to be parked towards the bow of the ship. If no deceleration was felt on touch down you immediately applied full power to go round accompanied by a shower of red flares and the cry of 'Bolter, bolter' from Flyco. You then rejoined the circuit for another go. Once the ship and her squadrons were fully worked up you would often find the ship still turning onto her designated flying course as you 'slotted', only steadying on the correct course as the first aircraft rolled out on final approach.

During my time embarked on *Victorious* the ship stayed east of Suez, operating mainly in the Far East. We visited Hong Kong, Subic Bay and Singapore regularly. The ship was getting old by this time and generally seemed to suffer some form of mechanical breakdown on an almost weekly basis, requiring repair work to be done in a major dockyard. In May 1967 it was time for the ship to return to the UK for a major refit. We sailed up the west coast of Malaya, flying all the time, then we crossed the Indian Ocean heading towards Aden. The British were in the process of withdrawing from Aden at this time and the security situation in the colony was very tense. Also in Aden at the time was HMS *Hermes*, the carrier that was to take over our role east of Suez. Thus there was a rare opportunity for two Royal Navy aircraft carriers to operate together for a short time. We spent three or four days flying around the Aden Protectorate, accompanied by Hunters from Khormaksar, in a display of airpower that was designed to impress upon the locals our capability to quell any unrest. This culminated in an enormous, unwieldy 55 aircraft flypast, consisting of all the serviceable Sea Vixens and Buccaneers from *Victorious* and *Hermes*, together with a large number of Hunters.

We bade farewell to *Hermes* and steamed up the Red Sea toward the Suez Canal, with canvas swimming baths rigged on the flight deck to cool off in, uncertain as to whether we would be able to transit through the canal. The Middle East was in turmoil, with the prospects of a war between Israel and the Arab nations becoming more likely every day. We listened to the BBC world service with great interest; the alternative route would have been all the way round South Africa. Nevertheless, we did go through the canal, but there were signs of military activity building up on both sides. We watched Egyptian Air Force pilots, who watched us from the bank, as we sailed slowly through. Eventually *Victorious* emerged into the Mediterranean where we continued to operate, somewhat restricted by the fact that there was no fleet tanker to replenish us. On the morning that the 1967 Arab/Israeli War broke out we sailed into Grand Harbour, Valletta, where we remained for the rest of that conflict despite Egyptian claims that we were assisting the Israelis. A postcard purchased some years later in Malta shows the carrier firmly anchored in Grand Harbour!

I disembarked from *Victorious* in the summer of 1967 and remained with 801 Squadron for another year, going back to sea for a short time before being posted to CFS to become a flying instructor. After a short time instructing on the Gnat I joined 736 NAS with two other pilots (Tim Cockerell and Jerry Yates) and three navigators (Barry Dove, Mick Whybro and Dave Laskey) who had all served on Navy Buccaneer squadrons. We were the team responsible for training the first eight courses of RAF aircrew, although in practice we were completely integrated with the Naval aircrew on the squadron; we flew equally with RN and RAF students. Eight old, and rather tired, Buccaneer S.1s were taken out of storage, maintained by the RAF and used for the RAF flying task, as there were insufficient numbers of S.2s to meet the extra flying.

My first task was to refresh and qualify as a QFI on the Hunter, our only dual control aircraft which was used for all early handling sorties and instrument flying. Our Hunters had the Buccaneer's flight instrument system installed on the left hand side for the student pilot. That apart, it shared no common handling characteristics with the Buccaneer and was much easier to fly. I also became an Instrument Rating Instructor (IRI), which involved a pleasant two week detachment down to RNAS Yeovilton to fly with the Naval Flying Standards Flight. Next, it was time to become checked out as a QFI on the Buccaneer. The QFI sat in the back seat, devoid of any flying controls and with minimal flight instruments to assist him. The view forward was quite good, especially on the right-hand side, as the seat was higher and offset to the right compared to the front seat. Thus you could monitor the progress of the sortie quite effectively, and provide advice, encouragement and remonstrations to the tyro pilot in the front, but there was no way of controlling the aircraft, The tyro pilot would complete at least six simulator rides, culminating in a complex emergencies sortie, and three trips in the Hunter. These three trips were very useful in that they gave the QFI a fair idea of his student's ability and competence. Then it was time for the FAM 1, the student's first Buccaneer sortie and also his first solo. Some of these sorties were nerve wracking events for both individuals

The sortie profile included a climb to height for some handling at around 30,000 ft with and without autostabilisation, a maximum rate descent to 10,000 ft for more handling and basic aerobatics, a descent to low level for a high speed run, then some practice at flying the aircraft in the landing configuration. Then it was back to the airfield for a long straight in approach, followed by visual circuits, culminating, hopefully, in a successful landing. If a major unserviceability occurred at a critical stage in the sortie, such as an engine failure on take-off or in the circuit, the chances of a successful outcome were remote and totally depended on the reactions of the student pilot. The S.1 version of the Buccaneer was particularly underpowered, and not very serviceable, so every FAM 1 was an exciting affair. Thereafter the QFI did not fly in the back again, handing over to an experienced staff observer/navigator, unless an individual was having particular difficulties on the early sorties. Apart from the FAM 1, the rest of the flying on 736 was fairly routine and typical of an operational conversion outfit. There were still quite a few RN aircrew going through and they enjoyed a longer and more comprehensive course than their RAF colleagues, including air-to-air refuelling, visual and photo reconnaissance and DLP.

The two years of RAF training passed very quickly and generally without major incidents. By the end of 1970 the last RAF course had arrived so the end of my association with the Fleet Air Arm was in sight and on 1 December I was scheduled to fly with Flying Officer Ivor Evans on his FAM 1 in XN951. By this time the S.1s were getting decidedly tired. Their Gyron Junior engines, never known for their user-friendly handling characteristics, were extremely difficult to accelerate in a crosswind on the runway. You often had to point directly into wind, brakes on, to persuade the engines to accelerate up to full power, then turn to line up with the runway as you started the take-off roll. The aircraft's acceleration was so sluggish that this evolution never presented any difficulty. Ominously on the FAM 1 we had great difficulty getting the port engine to accelerate through the inlet guide vane range before take-off but, with persistence, it finally wound up and off we went.

All went well until we returned to the circuit. We ended up too high and close on the first circuit so, at 200 ft, I told Ivor to overshoot and go round again. When he pushed the throttles forward for full power, all we got from the port engine was a lot of loud bangs and choking noises and no thrust. With commendable alacrity for a pilot on his first flight on type, Ivor lifted the wheels and got the airbrakes in, but with landing flap down and the blown ailerons and tailplane bleeding large amounts of air from the one good engine, Issac Newton's First Law soon kicked in. It very rapidly became evident that this sortie was not going to end satisfactorily without the help of Martin Baker's rocket-assisted deck chair. I had loosened my shoulder harness to see ahead, round the top of Ivor's ejection seat and this was no time to start tightening straps. Shouting EJECT, EJECT! I pulled the firing handle between my legs, and after a big bang I was looking down at the airfield grass coming up fast. I arrived on terra firma like a sack of spuds from a second floor window.

After establishing that I was alive and that my back hurt, my next priority was to get my Search and Rescue Beacon Equipment (SARBE) going to qualify for the silver tankard that the manufacturers gave to all aircrew that got to use their excellent product in a rescue. When an asbestos-suited fireman appeared in my field of vision I told him rudely to go away as I still hadn't got the beacon working. Given that I was sprawled in the middle of Lossiemouth airfield, he clearly thought I was delirious, took it gently from me and made soothing noises until the ambulance arrived. It transpired that Ivor had also jumped out successfully. The hapless Buccaneer had flopped on the airfield, narrowly missing some people mending a radar aerial, and had slithered to a halt on its belly on fire and with the cockpit section broken off. The big fire tender, when it finally arrived after getting bogged down in the grass, squirted foam all over it trying to extinguish the fire and shut down the starboard engine, which perversely continued running at full power for a while. A putrid smell drifted away on the wind and gave rise to serious complaints from lunchtime drinkers in the Wardroom.

I spent an uncomfortable three weeks lying flat on my back in hospital getting my vertebrae back in place, drinking smuggled whisky and annoying the nurses; in contrast, Ivor, whose straps were tight, was back flying in a couple of days. Barely a week after my accident a Buccaneer S.1 (XN968) which was being flown by two RAF students suffered a massive uncontained engine failure shortly after take-off. The pilot ejected successfully, but tragically the navigator (Pilot Officer P.J. Paines) was killed because a piece of perspex from the shattered canopy jammed the ejection seat's release mechanism and he was unable to separate himself from the seat in time. This accident brought Buccaneer S.1 flying to a halt for ever. Some of the remaining airframes were delivered to other airfields for use as Gate Guards or for battle damage repair work, the rest went to museums or scrap.

Tom Eeles continued his recuperation at Lossiemouth until March 1971 when he moved south to take up instructional duties at RAF Honington in Suffolk which was the home of the newly formed No.237 Operational Conversion Unit, the Buccaneer OCU. Although the Station Medical Officer insisted that he be grounded for a year following his spinal injuries, the back specialist at Ely hospital gave an altogether different opinion and Tom soon found himself back in the cockpit of a Buccaneer.

Pilot Debrief – 2

In March 1971 Tom Eeles began the first of his three tours with 237 OCU. He found that RAF Honington, with only 12 Squadron in residence at that time, was something of a 'sleepy hollow' compared with Lossiemouth, and that setting up the OCU was a considerable challenge with the need for a certain amount of ingenuity on his part to obtain everything that was needed. He recalls the early days of the OCU and one unfortunate incident during a night take off,

We opened for business in June 1971 and the pattern of activity was almost identical to what had taken place at Lossiemouth. Unfortunately there was no flight simulator at Honington so many journeys were made up north to use the simulator that was still in use at Lossie. Our early students were a complete mixture, ranging from first tourists with no previous experience through to our future Station Commander and even the Air Officer Commanding. The RAF looked on the Buccaneer as a sort of mini V-bomber and much to our horror tried to make us operate it in a similar fashion to a V-bomber. Not surprisingly we resisted as we saw the Buccaneer as more of a larger Hunter fighter-bomber. Luckily for us, our new Station Commander, Group Captain Peter Bairsto, known to all as 'The Bear', agreed with the maxi Hunter philosophy and fought hard for this in the corridors of power. The OCU was commanded by Wing Commander Anthony Fraser, his senior flight commander and Chief Flying Instructor being Squadron Leader David Mulinder. We soon settled into the business of training RAF aircrew on the Buccaneer and it was not long before some RN aircrew started to appear on the instructional staff.

On one particular night one of our first tour student navigators, David Herriot, and I were programmed to fly in a three aircraft formation, with us in the lead Buccaneer. Unusually it was a busy night at Honington, with a number of visiting aircraft including a twin-engined Andover that had brought in a load of VIPs. It was also a very dark night without moonlight or stars. All went well with the sortie up to the point when I lined up on the runway as a three aircraft formation for a 30 second stream take-off. Because of its naval ancestry, the Buccaneer was not equipped with a landing light, these being deemed superfluous on aircraft carriers, so it was not possible to see anything in the darkness ahead apart from the runway edge lighting. Brakes off, full power and off we went. All seemed OK to begin with, the airspeed indicator began to read but, at about 100 knots, the aircraft rapidly decelerated and came to a halt. I still had full power applied and thought at first I had inadvertently put the arrestor hook down, but the selector was in the UP position and there was no green light showing it to be down. Luckily none of the aircraft behind me had started their take-off roll so I called Air Traffic Control with a message that I 'seemed to have become stuck on the runway,' or words to that effect.

Air Traffic naturally assumed that I had put the hook down and had engaged the approach end of the arrestor cable as this had happened before. Doubtless thinking what idiots we were (you could tell from the tone of their voices) they sent a vehicle out to have a look at us. By this time I had throttled back to await developments. The vehicle approached, stopped a short distance away, then rapidly reversed out of the way. Air Traffic, now with a completely different tone of voice, told us to shut down but not to unstrap or attempt to get out until outside help had arrived. Eventually a team appeared from the darkness with an extending set of steps, which they gingerly placed by the cockpit. They then signalled us, from a distance, to get out. When we climbed down we saw that the arrestor cable was wrapped around the nosewheel leg. The whole thing was stretched tight like some giant catapult that appeared to be about to launch our Buccaneer backwards down the runway towards the rest of the formation who were still patiently sitting there.

By now the Bear, who was not noted for tolerance of professional foul ups, had arrived on the scene. Breathing fire from his nostrils he demanded to know precisely who was to blame for this shambles that had closed his airfield in such a thoughtless fashion, and in the middle of a VIP visit! Of course in the darkness of the night no one had a clue as to how this had happened or how to extract the aircraft from its imminent backwards launch. As the debate and argument continued amongst all parties out there on the runway the finger of suspicion seemed to be pointing more and more at my student and I. In the hubbub we both agreed it would be safer to make ourselves scarce and to slip away to the bar.

The answer to this saga only became clear the next morning. Lying on the grass beside the runway was found the shattered remains of a metal stand that the fire crews used to hold up the arrestor cable about 3 feet above the runway to allow them to move the rubber grommets that supported the cable more easily into position. Whilst re-rigging the cable after the arrival of the VIPs' Andover the night before, they were hassled by Air Traffic to hurry up as my formation was already taxiing. In their haste to get the job done they forgot to remove the stand. I then hit it on take off and inevitably collected the cable around the nosewheel leg. Amazingly there was little damage to the Buccaneer; it needed a new nosewheel leg and two new underwing tanks, but that was all. Not long afterwards all RAF Buccaneers were equipped with a landing light but whether this would have influenced the outcome is impossible to say.

On completion of his tour with the OCU Tom Eeles was then posted to 12 Squadron in June 1972. He was to fly the Buccaneer with 'Shiny Twelve' until March 1975,

No.12 Squadron had a new leader in Wing Commander Ian Henderson and there were a number of relatively new squadron members along with myself, so we all set to with a will. It was hard work. No. 12 Squadron's task was to provide maritime strike/attack capability to the Supreme Commander Atlantic (SACLANT); its secondary role was nuclear strike in support of the UK National Plan. Looking back in my logbook I see that I regularly flew 35 hours a month, a lot of it at night, with many detachments away from Honington. Within weeks of my arrival we were detached to Stornoway in the Hebrides as Lossiemouth's main runway was being repaired, for the big autumn exercise that always took place in the North Sea and Atlantic. We soon found ourselves flying as far south as Gibralter with the assistance of air-to-air refuelling.

Planning the flying programme on 12 Squadron was originally rather a 'hit and miss' business, with one or other of the numerous Squadron Leaders getting the task at short notice. With the complications of booking activities well ahead it was decided to give the programming job to two competent Flight Lieutenants as a full time commitment. Thus Bruce Chapple and I became the 12 Squadron programming and planning team, a busy and rewarding task. It also meant that we could both take advantage of the good deals when they came along, as long as we were not too obvious about it. One of these was a BBC TV Programme called *Skywatch*. This was a programme featuring all RAF activities including a firepower demonstration on

Salisbury Plain. No.12 Squadron's involvement was to provide four aircraft, each firing a full war load of 2 inch rockets with high explosive heads. This amounted to 144 rockets per aircraft, something which none of us had ever done before. Normally we simply went to the range and fired 9 rockets singly in an academic pattern; occasionally we would do a first run attack using an operational profile but merely firing a single rocket. Thus this exercise was a never to be repeated opportunity.

The target was a concrete tower about 20 feet high, surrounded by a group of redundant vehicles. We were told to take our time around the pattern and only fire when completely happy. When the moment came, it was astonishing. The whole of the area in front of the aircraft was obscured in smoke and rocket exhaust flame, there was a powerful stench of cordite in the cockpit and in spite of the fast ripple mode of fire being used it seemed to take forever for the rockets all to leave their launcher pods. Subsequent viewing of the video of what happened in the target area, which of course we did not see from the cockpit, was awe-inspiring. The concrete tower, which for years had withstood efforts by army artillery to destroy it, crumbled and disappeared. The vehicles were smashed to pieces and hurled about all over the place. Our opinion of the 2 inch rocket, which up to this point had been rather disparaging, suddenly improved by a large amount!

The other weapons available to us were really no different from many years previous. Our conventional bomb was the 1,000 lb high explosive bomb, which could be fitted with a retard or ballistic tail. For night illumination we had the Lepus flare which was tossed in a ballistic trajectory towards the target before deploying a parachute and igniting. Our conventional attack tactics had to be designed around these weapons. Thus we ended up with large formations of eight aircraft split into two sections of four each. One section was responsible for defence suppression, using a toss attack to throw a large number of air burst bombs towards the target in the hope that radar gun laying and missile guidance systems would be knocked off line. The other section would then close for an accurate shallow dive, level retard or rocket attack to finish off the target. Whether this would have worked out successfully for real was uncertain.

We spent many hours in the air co-ordinating these attacks and on a good day they worked out well. On a bad day, with poor weather, aircraft snags and poor communications, they could be a nightmare. Since they all involved getting very close to the target with no screening from the ship's defences we all felt very vulnerable. At night we reduced the aircraft numbers and used the Lepus flare to illuminate the target before carrying out a dive attack which was quite scary on a dark night, On one occasion I did succeed in sinking the splash target being towed by a frigate, very much to both my and the ship's amazement. Of course we also had the ultimate (nuclear) option but again the delivery aircraft would have been very vulnerable.

During my tour on 12 Squadron some welcome new equipment began to appear. During 1973 we began to receive the Martel missile system. It was designed as a defence suppression weapon in its anti-radar mode and a ship sinker in its TV mode. It was quite big, about 12 feet long, and the Buccaneer could carry four anti-radar, three TV missiles or a combination of both. The anti-radar version could be launched from low level about 20 miles from the target, it would climb to height then dive on to the target, exploding close to any radar it was locked onto. The TV version was launched at low level about 12 miles from the target. The launch aircraft could then turn away and, through a data-link pod, establish a TV and radio command link with the missile, which cruised at about 800 ft and 500 knots. The missile had a TV camera in its nose and the picture was displayed on a TV screen in the navigator's cockpit. The navigator could control the missile through a small control column and guide it with great accuracy into the target ship once it came in view. That, at least, was the theory.

The TV missile was thus limited to daylight and reasonably good weather but combined with its anti-radar version it did at last give us a reasonable stand-off attack capability. We were involved in the trial firings in Aberporth Range off the Welsh coast. On one occasion it was decided to combine a Martel firing with a trial to test whether a Phantom's radar could pick up a missile like Martel, which was similar in size to a number of Soviet missiles. There was a layer of cloud on the day from 1,500 ft to 2,500 ft so the Martel would be below this whilst the Phantom would be above. The missile was duly fired and set off towards the target; the Phantom was head on to it and cruising at 3,000 ft. The Phantom's navigator soon locked on to the Martel. Unfortunately as soon as the Buccaneer's navigator selected the terminal phase of the attack, his TV screen went blank and he lost all control of his Martel. Shortly afterwards the Martel shot out of the cloud going vertically upwards, narrowly missing the Phantom on both its upward and subsequent downward trajectory. It was decided not to repeat this trial again!

Many of our detachments were to Malta, Gibraltar and Cyprus for various exercises with the Royal Navy. I participated in a firepower demonstration in Cyprus when the first public demonstration of the BL755 cluster bomb took place, delivered from a Buccaneer flown by the Bear. Cyprus was invaded by the Turks in 1974; when this occurred I was on leave and for the first and only time in my career I was recalled. I was one of the last to get back to Honington and the first four crews were already walking to their aircraft to set off for Cyprus when I got into the squadron late that evening. They never got airborne and we spent the next three days hanging around in the expectation of going. Ultimately we were stood down and never went. However, there was an amusing sequel to all this.

One of our aircraft was in Engineering Wing undergoing a minor service. The staff, with commendable enthusiasm, worked day and night to get the aircraft serviceable quickly and it was soon delivered to the squadron. What we did not know was that the Engineering Wing staff had prepared it for an overseas deployment 'by the book'. This involved fitting a full set of aircraft access steps, intake blanks, ground locks and engineering manuals in the bomb bay, a considerable load. We on the squadron were not aware of this and as the bomb door was not rotated very often, it remained inside but unknown. A few days later we were involved in a demonstration to members of the Royal College of Defence Studies, very important people, who were embarked on a destroyer in the North Sea.

After carrying out our demo co-ordinated attack we re-formed for a low fast flypast over the ship. The formation leader, the Boss, briefed that we should all open our bomb doors just as we approached the ship, as this action made a wonderful noise. Imagine my surprise when I saw his door open and the ladders, locks, intake blanks and manuals all fall out. Luckily, given their poor ballistic qualities, they fell into the sea well short of the destroyer but the Navy and College staff and students were equally astonished. I understand that there was a tense exchange of signals between the Royal Navy and RAF Honington on the incident.

After nearly three years with 12 Squadron the RAF's posting people caught up with Tom Eeles again and he was dispatched to the Tactical Weapons Unit at Brawdy to fly Hunters. His next stint on Buccaneers was back at 237 OCU from January 1977 to January 1980 and on this tour he became the unit's Chief Flying Instructor,

The OCU was now a busy place. There were two squadrons (12 and 208) based at Honington, two more based at Laarbruch (15 and 16) and the last RN squadron (809) which was still in commission and based at Honington when not at sea in *Ark Royal*. Thus there was a constant stream of aircrew, both new and experienced, to put through the course. No. 237 OCU had a reputation for being a hard outfit to get through, particularly for aircrew that had come from the V force. However, with no dual control version of the Buccaneer we had to insist on high standards and we were no harder on our students than the RN had been back on 736 Squadron. It seemed that many expected an easier ride than they got and so complained when they found the going tough. My opposite number as Senior Nav Instructor was Dick Moore, a Cranwell contemporary who had gone on to Hunters but who had unfortunately lost an eye when a bird came through the canopy of his aircraft. He had retrained as a navigator and was a very good one. Our boss was Wing Commander Arnie Parr, who was a hard taskmaster. Inevitably I spent a lot of time in the Hunter, with the associated FAM 1s in the Buccaneer, but as a Flight Commander there was now the chance to pinch one or two of the more enjoyable trips, such as the 'Bounce' for strike progression sorties.

The pressure to produce trained crews was relentless and the conditions for doing so were far less suitable than they had been up at Lossiemouth. Limited availability of weapons ranges and poor weather were the two principal limiting factors that bedevilled our activities. Our safety record was remarkably good. We had one fatal accident involving our Naval pilot, who, when away in Norway for a weekend overseas training flight, decided to undertake some illegal low flying up a fjord on his way home, despite the protestations of his RAF navigator. He flew into high tension cables and lost control; both ejected but only the navigator survived [this incident occurred on 31 October 1977 and involved XV348].

Another less traumatic, but nevertheless dramatic incident occurred when a student crew set off on a routine sortie to the Wash bombing ranges. The Buccaneer's pre-take-off checks included a check by the pilot that the canopy was both closed and locked – the locking action being a separate selection to closing. The navigator observed that the aircraft was very noisy as they transited over Norfolk at 250 ft and 420 kts – the first clue that all was not well but it was missed. Once out over the sea the pilot accelerated to 550 kts to trim the aircraft out at his attack speed. He then turned towards the range. At this point the canopy, which the pilot had failed to lock in his pre-take-off checks, finally gave up and was ripped off the aircraft, embedding itself deep into the fin. The cockpit was filled with dust and a 550 knot breeze; the poor navigator could not move or speak but the pilot, protected by the front windscreen, was a bit better off. They slowed down, put out a distress call then elected to return all the way to Honington. I was the duty instructor at the time. I was summoned to the ATC tower and eventually the aircraft came into view, escorted by a passing Jaguar. It presented an amazing sight, as the canopy was a very substantial piece of equipment and it was stuck halfway into the fin. Apparently this highly unusual configuration did not significantly affect the aircraft's handling characteristics!

The summer of 1977 marked the 25th anniversary of the Queen's accession to the throne so it was decided to put twenty-five RAF aircraft into the flypast over Buckingham Palace at the end of the Trooping of the Colour Parade. The formation was to consist of two Vulcans, two Victors, two Buccaneers, two Lightnings, four Jaguars, four Phantoms and nine Red Arrows Gnats. This disparate collection of aircraft, with widely differing performances and fuel states, was to be led by a Vulcan whose captain had virtually no experience of formation flying, let alone leading mixed formations over London at low level. The whole unwieldy formation was to fly at 240 kts, a ridiculously low speed for the fast jets but chosen for time keeping purposes; the V-bombers were limited to remain below 300 kts at low level. The forecast on the day was for deteriorating weather over London but the pressure was on for us to be there. We all formed up over Southwold and set off towards London flying at about 1,000 ft above ground level. All went well at first, but as we approached the suburbs the cloud base started to get lower and lower. With the lead Vulcan at 1,000 ft, the rest were all stepped down behind him so that the Red Arrows right at the back were down at about 600 ft over the buildings of the East End. It was a hairy ride as it was getting turbulent.

By the middle of London the cloud base was down to 1,000 ft and the lead Vulcan was at 800 ft, putting the Reds down at around 400 ft. Just after passing the Palace, all mayhem broke loose. The rearmost Victor, with two Phantoms on each side, got too close to the Victor ahead and pushed down to avoid collision, thereby putting itself right in the face of the Gnats. At the same moment the leading Vulcan went into cloud. The Reds broke away, descended as low as they dared and raced off over west London back to their home base at Kemble. The Jaguars, Lightnings and Phantoms, by now in cloud, all broke away from their V-bombers, engaged afterburners and split up, climbing for safety in the middle of the busy London Control Zone. I and my No.2 managed to stick on the wing of our Vulcan as it stumbled up through

HMS *Ark Royal* with Buccaneer S.2s of 809 Squadron in the foreground and Phantoms of 892 Squadron to the rear. (via Philip Jarrett)

Buccaneer S.2 XN975 shortly before touchdown on HMS *Ark Royal* during deck landing trials in March 1965. (Crown Copyright via Philip Jarrett)

Three Buccaneer S.2s of 809 Squadron from HMS *Hermes* fly along the coastline of Aden on 14 May 1967 during passage to the Far East. (via Philip Jarrett)

T281, one of the Buccaneer S.2s of 809 Squadron that took part in the 1968 Farnborough Air Show, dumps fuel prior to landing. (via Philip Jarrett)

Buccaneer S.2 fast and low over the sea. (Crown Copyright via Philip Jarrett)

Buccaneer S.2 XV865 of 736 Squadron from Lossiemouth carries a rocket launcher on the port inr pylon. (via Philip Jarrett)

A Buccaneer S.2 of 809 Squadron lands on HMS *Ark Royal*. (via Philip Jarrett)

ocket firing in Buccaneer S.2 XT285 of 736 Squadron. This aircraft was subsequently modified for the ornado development programme but was lost when it stalled and crashed at West Freugh on 5 July 978. (Crown Copyright via Philip Jarrett)

Buccaneer S.2 about to catch a wire on HMS *Hermes*. (via Philip Jarrett)

Buccaneer S.2 XV152 with airbrakes partially deployed. (via Philip Jarrett)

A Buccaneer S.2 of 809 Squadron leaves the deck of HMS *Hermes*. (via Philip Jarrett)

Eight 1,000 lb bombs are released from a Royal Navy Buccaneer S.2 during Unison '67. (via Philip Jarrett)

Two Buccaneer S.2s of 801 Squadron take on fuel from Victor K.1 XH650 during the rehearsal for Unison '67. (via Philip Jarrett)

Anyone who was at the Farnborough Air Show in 1968 (including the author) will long remember the Royal Navy demonstration, particularly the finale which included near sonic flypasts by six Sea Vixens, four Phantoms and five Buccaneers, including XT280 of 809 Squadron. (via Philip Jarrett)

Long term development aircraft XK527 takes a wire during landing at RAE Bedford. (RAE Bedford via Philip Jarrett)

Buccaneer S.2 XV351 of 12 Squadron in the overrun area at Karup after a take-off accident on 12 May 1971. The navigator's parachute is in the foreground. (via author)

Buccaneer S.2 XT270 of 12 Squadron fires rockets from underwing SNEB pods. (Crown Copyright via Philip Jarrett)

In the early 1970s external bomb loads of up to twelve 1,000 lb bombs were contemplated. XW525 is seen here with eight 1,000 lb bombs during manufacturer's trials. It later served with the RAF and crashed on 27 April 1977 when control was lost avoiding a Hunter over Wales. (via Philip Jarrett)

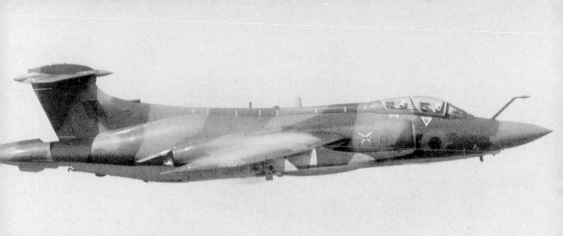

Buccaneer S.2 wearing the crossed swords of 237 OCU. (via Philip Jarrett)

Martel equipped Buccaneer at the Hanover Air Show in 1974. The data link pod is carried on the port inner pylon. (via Philip Jarrett)

Hawker Siddeley test pilot Don Headley flies XK527 fitted with four Martel missiles. The pilot of th[e] photographic aircraft refused to manoeuvre around XK527 so Don had to do all the work himself! (v[ia] Philip Jarrett)

Another view of XK527 with Martel missiles. (via Philip Jarrett)

After service with the Royal Navy and RAF, Buccaneer S.2 XV350 was used for manufacturer's trials and is seen here with four Martel missiles. (via Philip Jarrett)

Buccaneer S.2 XT279 of 16 Squadron in December 1983 in all black scheme with yellow 'Saint' emblem. (via Philip Jarrett)

XW988 was used as a trials machine by MoD and is seen here in a yellow and green high visibility pai
scheme. (RAE Bedford via Philip Jarrett)

Buccaneer S.2 XX893 of XV Squadron low over Germany. (Crown Copyright via Philip Jarrett)

V161 and XV354 of 208 Squadron low over the sea. (via Philip Jarrett)

ıccaneer S.2 XT280 of 208 Squadron carries four Sea Eagle missiles and displays the bomb door fuel ık which extended the Buccaneer's already excellent range. (via Philip Jarrett)

XX897 was another MoD trials aircraft which was modified with the nose and radar of a Tornado F.2. (RAE Bedford via Philip Jarrett)

thick turbulent cloud; the cloud was so dense that I could only see a small portion of the Vulcan's enormous wing. It was the most frightening situation I had been in for a long time, especially as we were flying so slowly. We had no idea what had happened to the rest of the formation. Eventually we broke out of cloud somewhere to the north of London, only to see the Vulcan that had originally been behind us out ahead by a mile or so. Somehow it had overtaken us in cloud, how close it had come we will never know. We recovered back to Honington thankful that we had survived and I swore never to get involved in flypasts over London again, a commitment I was unable to honour. The photo taken from the ground as we flew over the Palace does not show the chaos that was about to occur.

During this tour the Royal Navy finally finished fixed-wing flying in 1978 and our small RN Unit was disbanded. The 809 Squadron aircraft were handed back to the RAF, repainted in RAF colours and another squadron (216) was expected to form at Honington. Coincidental with this unit's re-formation was the introduction of another new weapon system into the Buccaneer inventory, the Pave Spike laser designation pod and the laser guided bomb (LGB). The introduction of this equipment did not affect our activities on 237 OCU at this time but it would do in the future. In 1977 the first RAF participation in the USAF's Red Flag exercise took place, again a first for the Buccaneer. We sent our Qualified Weapons Instructor course along on the first Red Flag, along with an instructor crew. The Americans were astonished at the way in which the British operated their aircraft and were somewhat mortified to find that our tactics were extremely successful when compared to their own.

In 1979, as my time on 237 OCU was coming to an end, the first fatal accident involving structural failure of a Buccaneer wing occurred. In this incident the latch pin, which held the folding section of the wing in place, failed on a German-based aircraft. All latch pins were replaced and the fleet was soon flying again, but not for long. In February 1980 there was another fatal accident during a Red Flag exercise; in this case the wing failed in the inner non-folding section due to metal fatigue. The whole fleet was grounded with little prospect of an early return to flying status. Thus it was not too hard a pill to swallow when I left Honington for the now inevitable desk jobs; at least it was to be via a year at the RAF Staff College at Bracknell.

While Tom Eeles went off to fly a desk for a while, the Buccaneer fleet was drastically reduced in size and 216 Squadron which had re-formed on 1 July

1979 was disbanded once again. By the time that he returned to 237 OCU in August 1984, this time as its Commanding Officer, the Buccaneer force had been trimmed even further with XV and 16 Squadrons in Germany re-equipping with the Tornado GR.1. During his third tour at the OCU Tom was to receive a special patch to adorn his flying suit to mark his 2,000th hour on the Buccaneer,

By early 1984 the Buccaneer Force had changed considerably from what it had been when I left it in early 1980. After the wing failure accident in the USA the number of serviceable aircraft had reduced significantly and there were only enough for two front line squadrons and an OCU. The two remaining squadrons (12 and 208) were now both based at Lossiemouth and were committed specifically to the maritime attack role. The OCU was still located at Honington but was due to move late in 1984 to join the squadrons at Lossiemouth. I started my refresher flying in May 1984 and almost immediately got involved with a Board of Inquiry into a fatal accident that occurred on 208 Squadron. Once that was over I completed my refresher and took over the unit from the indefatigable Wing Commander David Mulinder in September. No sooner had I taken command, when arrangements for us to move north really began to gather pace.

One thing I will never forget was our Dining Out from Honington. The boys constructed a large Buccaneer made out of cardboard, about eight feet long, equipped with a rocket launching tube under each wing. A long electrical cable connected the launching tubes to a 12 volt car battery. An initial trial firing in the empty squadron building was truly spectacular, with the rockets exploding violently on impact with the wall. The reaction to this was that it was too dangerous to use it in the Officer's Mess, but, after a few beers before the event, the boys changed their mind and it was duly suspended from the ceiling of the dining room, with the car battery hidden beneath the table. Despite the attempts of the Mess Staff to have it removed, it survived and we all sat down to dine with it hanging menacingly over us. On my left was the Boss of the Tornado Weapons Conversion Unit. He asked what the Buccaneer was going to do – I explained that it would be pulled along the rail from which it was suspended and that it would dump a large amount of talcum powder on whoever was below – which happened to be him. He was not amused and we didn't converse very much for the rest of the evening. On my right was OC Ops Wing. He too asked what the Buccaneer would do – I told him to get down under the table as soon as I had completed my speech – good advice as it turned out.

When my turn came to speak, I made an appropriately rabble rousing speech vilifying the Tornado and extolling the virtues of the Buccaneer. When I finished speaking the switch was thrown on the battery, there was a suitably theatrical pause, which convinced diners that it wasn't going to work, then the rockets went off. They spread all over the dining room, exploding loudly wherever they hit. How no one was injured I will never know. About three or four hit the door leading to the kitchens, which was severely damaged as a consequence. Behind the door was a lady carrying a large tray of glasses from the dishwasher to the cupboards; when the rockets struck she dropped the entire tray load and screamed loudly, thereby enhancing the whole effect of the event. The whole dining room erupted with a standing ovation, which was most gratifying and a fitting way to end the Buccaneer's association with RAF Honington. The rest of the evening has disappeared from my memory in an alcoholic haze, but inscribed in my logbook is the following statement, written by the Station Commander, Group Captain Peter Harding – 'As 237 OCU is re-located at RAF Lossiemouth, the Buccaneer era comes to an end at Honington after 15 years. My best wishes to you and 237 for a successful time at Lossiemouth, thank you for all your help both in the air and on the ground during a trouble free move north. We shall remember the Guest Night for ever, the scars will not remain for quite so long.'

Being in charge of 237 OCU at Lossiemouth was a great pleasure. The weather factor was very good, we had weapons ranges right on the door step, the vast low flying area in the north of Scotland was always available and I had an excellent team of instructors and ground crew. Although all the Buccaneer squadrons belonged to 18 Group, the maritime element of Strike Command, 237 OCU was given an interesting and unique war role, which had nothing to do with maritime operations. When the Buccaneer squadrons were withdrawn from RAF Germany in 1984 there was no unit in that theatre of operations that could undertake airborne laser designation for aircraft carrying laser guided bombs. There were a number of important operational plans that required the use of airborne laser designation, so as 237 OCU had a number of very experienced overland Buccaneer navigators, it was given the task of supporting the Jaguar and Tornado squadrons in Germany in war time. This required regular visits to Laarbruch to work with the resident squadrons. Not surprisingly HQ 18 Group were not particularly enthusiastic about this activity as it would have liked to have had all Buccaneers assigned to maritime operations, but we were determined to carry on with this work, ably supported in HQ 2ATAF by Group Captain Nigel Walpole who was a great enthusiast for our overland capabilities. It also gave the squadron a unique ethos, which was much preferable to supporting the other two squadrons at Lossiemouth.

A by-product of this activity was the opportunity to become involved in the NATO squadron exchange scheme. A Dutch F-16 squadron (322) based at Leeuwarden, was equipped to carry LGBs and with the assistance of Nigel Walpole we organised an exchange with them. The Dutch were keen to toss some of their LGBs at Garve Island, the Cape Wrath weapons range, as there was nowhere in Holland where they could do this. We were naturally going to provide the laser designation for them, thereby giving a graphic demonstration of true NATO interoperability. Two Buccaneers and two F-16s set off for Garve, the weather was good and I had an expert Pave Spike operator, Norman Browne, as my navigator. The live toss bombing exercise was a great success with all the F-16s bombs guiding well and impacting on target. Norman even managed to organise an HF radio link to Nigel Walpole in his office in Germany to tell him of our success. It was a case of so far, so good.

The plan was then to fly across the 'moon country' in the north of Scotland, escorted by the two F-16s, to be bounced by a third F-16. The 'bounce' duly turned up, our two Buccaneers accelerated off leaving the three Dutchman to indulge in a bit of air combat. Half an hour later we were sitting in the debrief, watching the Pave Spike videos when a broadcast from ATC announced that an F-16 was returning to the circuit with engine handling problems….it was our bounce aircraft that had got airborne somewhat later than us. A few moments later ATC confirmed that the aircraft had landed safely and we went back to debrief. Suddenly, the door to the briefing room burst open, revealing an incandescent F-16 pilot, gibbering away in what can only be described as Double Dutch. All the remaining Dutchmen immediately leapt to their feet and rushed out upstairs to their detachment office, slamming the door shut behind them. Sounds of considerable altercation came from behind the closed door. At this point my Warrant Officer, Jack Sim, sidled up to me – 'I think you had better come out to the flight line and have a look at this F-16,' he said. The F-16 sat there, a thin wisp of vapour coming out of its jet pipe. Closer inspection revealed that the entire back end of the aircraft was riddled with 20 mm bullet holes. 'Get it into the hangar as quick as you can' I said to Jack.

By now the Dutch had calmed down somewhat and were able to offer an explanation. After leaving the bombing range one of the pilots had failed to put his master armament switch to safe. F-16s always flew with a full load of 20 mm ball ammunition to keep the CG within limits. Our pilot found himself in a position to claim a shot at the F-16 ahead of him, he selected air-to-air, pressed the trigger to film his opponent, and because his master arm switch was still live, the gun fired. Luckily he was only tracking the rear of the aircraft ahead, not the cockpit as is normal. However, seeing that nothing appeared amiss with his opponent, he decided to say nothing and carried on with the fight! His opponent, unaware of what had happened, carried on with his sortie and only became aware that something was not quite right when he rejoined the circuit. The Dutch decided to lock up their miscreant pilot in the detachment office for the rest of the day/night.

I went to see the Station Commander, Group Captain Bruce Latton, to brief him on the affair. His immediate and understandable reaction was that we should tell someone but I urged caution. After all, the incident had taken place over moon country and was unlikely to have been witnessed by anyone. The Dutch were doubtless going to take care of their culprit in their own way. If anyone brought in a dead sheep riddled with 20 mm, or even a dead human, we could always claim that the incident was under investigation. Eventually the Station Commander agreed and we left it to the Dutch to sort out. The unfortunate pilot was flown back to Holland the next day in handcuffs and the F-16 underwent an engine change in our hangar. No one from moon country complained and the incident was quietly forgotten, however, I could not resist mentioning at the final Dining In Night that when the RAF shot themselves down they did it properly! [In 1982 a 92 Squadron Phantom had shot down a Jaguar GR.1 of 14 Squadron with a Sidewinder missile as it was recovering to Bruggen in Germany. The pilot of the Jaguar ejected safely]. Our next squadron exchange was with a Portuguese Air Force squadron and was an altogether much more restrained affair. [For the full story of Tom Eeles' long RAF career, see *A Passion For Flying* also published by Pen and Sword Books Ltd.]

CHAPTER FOURTEEN

Pilot Debrief – 3

During his time as Station Commander at RAF Honington from 1980-82, Group Captain Mike Shaw managed to accumulate around 300 hours on the Buccaneer which was slightly more time than he had been able to record in his logbook during his first tour on Lightnings with 74 Squadron in the early 1960s! The early part of his command unfortunately coincided with the fatigue problems that had become apparent after the crash of a Buccaneer in the USA whilst taking part in the USAF Red Flag exercise. All Buccaneers were immediately grounded and many were found to have serious fatigue in the inner wing spar. This was to cause serious problems for the Buccaneer force as he recalls,

My Buccaneer conversion was unfortunately curtailed by the wing falling off in Nevada and so I never actually completed the course; instead they gave me an honorary pass. For the first four months of my command at Honington I never flew a Buccaneer and neither did anybody else, so I had a station of eight Hunters. One of the main problems at the time was that the navigators did not get much flying. They went in the right-hand seat of the Hunter but it wasn't at all the same as being in a Buccaneer. Some of the Hunters were T.8s which had the Integrated Flight Instrument System (IFIS) in front of the pilot, which I felt was actually a worse system than the original flight instrumentation in the Hunter. We had to fly them because they were more like a Buccaneer, but I personally thought that they were a waste of time. We made full use of the simulators and because we were not allowed to fly our Buccaneers they became even more important than usual. These gave great confidence when we were checked out in that we knew we would be able to cope in an emergency. This was important not only for myself, but as Station Commander I had a responsibility for every other pilot and navigator at Honington. If somebody had pranged, it was my station and the buck stopped with me. Fortunately we did not lose anybody while I was there.

We had a Station Commander's Mineval which was a kind of practice war every six weeks to keep us prepared for the Taceval

(Tactical Evaluation) that was meant to occur once a year. We would be descended upon by a whole horde of people who, of course, never notified you that they were on their way. A usual trick was to appear on a Sunday night when you had half the ground crew off station for the weekend. The aim was to get the minimum number of aircraft combat ready on the flight line and with crews, all within a 12 hour deadline. The only unit on the station that was Taceval-able by the time I had been there for a year was 208 Squadron, the OCU did not take part as it was not declared as an operational squadron. We always passed but they did land us with some difficult trips. I remember on one occasion that 208 Squadron were sent off to Norway with no notice. It was not easy to go off in the middle of a UK winter to land on a frozen runway in Norway. We always got everyone back in one piece but it was a bit of a tense time.

During the summer months we provided aircraft for various air displays around the country and I remember getting into trouble on one occasion when we sent six Buccaneers up to Waddington. They were from 208 Squadron and they were to perform an airfield attack which involved one pass followed by a rapid withdrawal. At that time some of the squadron pilots had been cleared down to 100 ft and as all the pilots taking part in the display had received the necessary authorisation I thought it would be good for Waddington if they did the simulated attack at 100 ft. This type of attack was normally carried out in pairs with each pair flying over the airfield at high speed from different directions at 10 second intervals. Unfortunately for me it turned out that the AOC had decided to drop in to watch the display.

I received a phone call from the Wing Commander Operations at Waddington who congratulated us on doing an excellent show and he said that everyone had really enjoyed it. I then contacted the Officer on our Operations desk and asked him to pass on Waddington's congratulations to the crews as they came in. The phone then rang again and it was the AOC who appeared to have been the only one not to have appreciated what we had done. He demanded to know who had authorised the display and so I informed him that it had been my decision. When he demanded to know what I had been thinking about I reminded him that the pilots had been given clearance down to 100 ft about a month previously and that he had approved it. He then said, 'Well yes, but not for air displays' to which I replied, 'Well, Sir, you didn't put a caveat on to say that they were cleared down to 100 ft but not for display flying!' I felt it was all a bit unfair but it eventually blew over and I didn't hear any more about it. The fact that the crews and the aircraft were up to a certain job was not, it would appear, terribly relevant. There was no real danger, although it must have been pretty spectacular.

Although Mike Shaw had a reputation for being one of the more active of the RAF's Station Commanders and was regularly to be seen in the cockpit of a Buccaneer during his time in charge at Honington, one particular sortie in 1982 was to prove that old habits die hard,

> I was in a pair of Buccaneers going across the North Yorkshire moors towards the weapons range at Cowden. On the way two Lightnings bounced us which I thought was a bit punchy and quite wrong. My natural reaction was to break in hard towards them, and when I did the pilot of the other Buccaneer must have been wondering what on earth I was doing. My navigator certainly did because he was a dyed-in-the-wool Buccaneer man and I wasn't really. I managed to get in behind one of the Lightnings which I was extremely pleased about. At that time we were not carrying the AIM-9G Sidewinder missile which, of course, the Buccaneer subsequently did. If I had been so equipped then that would have been enough to get the Lightning. The inevitable happened of course as the other Lightning got behind me and sandwiched me in but there was not much I could do about that. At least I got a bit of satisfaction out of it; I had fought back and I felt that honours were even. The Buccaneer could do that and even then I never got anywhere near overstressing it because we knew that wings could fall off Buccaneers by then and we preferred not to put that to the test. My navigator gave me a hard time over what I had done as he considered that I should have continued at low level directly towards the target. I am sure that he felt like reminding me that I wasn't a fighter pilot any more, but was probably too polite to mention it!

The most frightening trip that Mike Shaw experienced in a Buccaneer occurred during his conversion to type, a mere five weeks after his first familiarisation flight. On 20 December 1979 he was flying XT287 on a strike progression sortie with Flight Lieutenant 'Rattie' Adams as his navigator. For the time of year the weather conditions were quite good with a cloud base of 2,000 ft and a visibility of around 15 miles. As he was preparing to carry out a laydown attack he became aware that all was not well with his aircraft,

> The first thing I noticed was that my speed brakes did not come out when I selected them. These worked via a hydraulic system which for

some reason had suddenly failed. I then called the other aircraft that I was flying with but did not receive a reply. I found that I could talk to my navigator but not to anyone else as the radio was dead. There was an emergency radio with just the emergency frequency and one other, but when I called up on this there was still no reply. So I had no radios or hydraulics and I could not make out why. The hydraulics were not supposed to go to the emergency mode unless the pilot had selected an emergency system and I had not. At this time I was about 50-60 miles from Honington and so I decided to return immediately. I assumed that the other Buccaneer crew would make the necessary R/T calls to tell them I was coming and this they did.

I flew back and lined the aircraft up for a straight-in approach but due to the hydraulic failure I had to blow the flaps down by using the emergency system. The only problem with this was that once you had put the flaps down you could not raise them again. The aircraft was then in the fully blown configuration with the main flaps at 45 degrees, the ailerons drooped to 25 degrees, with the tailplane flap up 25 degrees. The situation then got a whole lot worse as my navigator informed me that the bomb-bay temperature gauge was off the clock. The maximum temperature on the gauge was 150 degrees C and apparently the pointer was hard up against the stop. This was a particular concern as the Buccaneer had eight fuel tanks mounted in the centre section directly above the bomb bay and by now the rearmost pair would have been empty and full of fumes. By this stage of the flight I was quite convinced that the back of the aeroplane was on fire.

Having set up the Buccaneer in the landing configuration I then got a further shock as I discovered that there was a serious loss of pitch control. Every time I pulled the stick back a little bit, if the tailplane negative angle of attack increased, it tended to stall. There were then two distinct possibilities, I might either dive into the ground or have the back end blown off at any moment, all of which added a fair bit of tension to the final approach. I was watching for the bomb-bay fire warning light to come on because if it did the crew had five seconds to get out. For the last ten miles or so I was watching for that light and I was conscious of the fact that an ejection was highly probable. Thankfully it did not come on and I was able to continue my approach to engage the arrestor wire at the upwind end of the runway.

When I got out of the aircraft I was shaking like a leaf and could barely stand. The Buccaneer looked perfect until they rotated the bomb door when all sorts of debris fell out of it. The interior was a complete mess. It transpired that the emergency had been caused by a failure of the BLC pipe that supplied hot air to the underside of the tailplane. This had fractured in the bomb bay and had burnt through the hydraulic lines leading to the airbrake. As the hydraulic system operated at about 4,000 psi it would not have taken long for all the fluid to disappear. It also meant that the bomb bay was then full of hydraulic fluid which was very inflammable. The lack of blow on the underside of the tailplane was the reason for the problems in pitch as the down load on the tail was much reduced. All the problems I had experienced were linked but at the time I could not make out exactly what was happening. I was convinced that I must have had a fire somewhere, as it turned out it was not quite as bad as that but it was getting close to it.

Although it had suffered serious internal damage, XT287 was repaired and later flew with XV Squadron in whose service it carried the name 'MacRobert's Reply', the name carried by a Short Stirling in the Second World War. It also went on to fly with 12 and 16 Squadrons and 237 OCU once again, before being scrapped at Lossiemouth on 12 May 1992. Incidents such as that recounted above could be set against lighter moments, one of which caused a certain amount of embarrassment for the Boss of 208 Squadron,

Two Buccaneers were going up to Lossiemouth to take part in the Tactical Bombing Competition in 1981 and in the back seat of one was the commander of 208 Squadron, Wing Commander Graham Pitchfork. Their suitcases were duly loaded up in a crate in the bomb bay of one of the Buccaneers and off they went. To make the maximum use of the air time the decision had been taken to go through one of the weapons ranges on the way to carry out a simulated toss bombing attack. This normally involved doing a half loop during which the bomb was released at a certain angle so that it was lobbed onto the target. Unfortunately they had forgotten about the load they were carrying and the Squadron Commander's suitcase did a nice parabola onto the target, although as its ballistic qualities left something to be desired I understand that it fell rather short. The pilot realised what he had done and quickly closed the bomb doors but it was too late, it had gone. After landing at Lossiemouth they went into the bar where, so the story goes, they were confronted by the Station Commander who at that time was Group Captain Sandy Wilson. He expressed his commiserations at the loss of the suitcase and its contents in the sea but then said, 'Don't worry Graham, we've recovered a bit of it.' He then produced a wringing wet pair of knickers and said, 'There you are at least you've got part of your belongings back!'

Wing Commander Pitchfork's embarrassment continued even after he returned to Honington when he discovered that the wives had made a large banner which had then been attached to 208 Squadron's hangar. It read 'Tactical Baggage Competition, 1981'.

Buccaneer Test Pilot

T he flight test programme for the Buccaneer was carried out from Holme-on-Spalding Moor, a former 4 Group bomber base which had been taken over by Blackburn Aircraft in 1957 from the USAF. This airfield was approximately ten miles north-west of Blackburn's production base at Brough and offered much better facilities and longer runways. Use was also made of another ex-bomber airfield at Elvington near York, the runway of which had been extended in the 1950s to 9,800 ft in length. One of the pilots involved in testing the Buccaneer was Don Headley who joined Hawker Siddeley (later BAe) on 1 January 1968 and was to be involved with the aircraft as a test pilot for the next fifteen years. He took over the role of Chief Test Pilot at Brough and Holme-on-Spalding Moor in 1975 and also took part in the development of the British version of the McDonnell Douglas Phantom. Before this he was a member of the Royal Navy Civilian Ferry Flight which involved delivering all types of naval aircraft to various military establishments throughout the UK.

I was delivering a Buccaneer to Aldergrove in Northern Ireland for servicing and on the way I had a hydraulic failure on the general services system. There was not too much to worry about but I called up to request that someone come out to the runway to put pins in the undercarriage before I taxied in, just to make sure. After landing they asked me to turn off onto a disused runway. I was then asked to stop but on no account was I to make any attempt to get out of the cockpit. They kept repeating this and eventually a Land Rover came out and a ladder appeared at the side. Even then the Tower told me to stay where I was and it was a couple of minutes later that they said 'You are cleared to get out of the cockpit.' By this time everything was shut down and as I was climbing down the ladder an Irish voice said 'Now when you get to the bottom of the ladder sir, just you make sure you stand in this tray of disinfectant as we're not having Foot and Mouth in Ireland.' To this day I don't think pins ever went in the undercarriage!

On another occasion I went to collect a Buccaneer from the Maintenance Unit at Aldergrove. After start-up the hydraulic warning sounded off and was also shown on the warning panel. The gauges were showing there was pressure but I shut the engines down and got out. The foreman came up and asked what was wrong and so I told him. He asked if there had been pressure on the gauges, so I said that there had been. To this he said 'Well that's all right then, you can take it' to which I replied 'No I can't.' His argument was that as there had been pressure on the gauges it was obviously a fault on the warning. Unfortunately he could not see the logic I was trying to get over to him, which was how would I have known if there had been a failure on the way when there was nothing to warn me. The Irish were a great bunch of people but with a completely different outlook on life.

On 3 October 1967 I was to deliver a Buccaneer (XV351) to Lossiemouth. At the time Hawker Siddeley were using Driffield as Holme-on-Spalding Moor was having concrete ends put in on the runway prior to the arrival of the Phantom. Derek Whitehead, the Chief Test Pilot, took me to one side and said that he had heard that there was a chance that Ferry Flight would be closing as the Navy had scrubbed a carrier. He was short of a production test pilot and offered me the job (it had been offered to Dave Eagles but he could not come as he was unable to get out of the Navy). If I agreed they would let me have use of the company Dove to get my Instrument Rating and they would back me to get a commercial licence, as on Ferry Flight you could operate on an ordinary PPL. I thought it was worth a gamble and said I would take it. My first production test in a Buccaneer was in XV358 on 17 January 1968.

Production testing on a particular aeroplane was normally completed in three flights although it could go up to five if there was a recurring problem. We had to check all the speeds and the full weapon system. Although we did not go through all the attack modes, we had to make sure that the weapon system came up with the right information. We took the aeroplane to the limits which included recording the maximum speed. On a normal day at 1,000 ft this was somewhere around 618 knots which was then cut back to the service limit of 580 knots. There was a very good reason for this as above 580 knots you started getting unannounced yaws on the aeroplane because of asymmetric movement of the shock wave on the rudder. Above 590-600 knots the aeroplane would suddenly lurch one way. There would then be an almighty bang as a result of an intake stall on the engine. Even though you got used to it, it still made you jump as 600 knots at 1,000 ft over the sea feels very fast.

With each new aeroplane that came along we had to do fuel

jettisoning. The Buccaneer had an automatic cut off so that all the fuel did not disappear out of the vent pipe. It would be highly illegal today but we used to fly over the airfield so that the Tower could tell us the precise point when the fuel actually stopped coming out. Alternatively, if the weather was right you could use the sun and the shadow of the aeroplane to see the actual cut-off point.

The only incident I had on a production flight was once when I took off in a brand new Buccaneer on its first flight. Immediately after take off it started pitching and yawing. My first reaction was 'What the hell is happening', but my next thought was to switch off the auto-stabilisers. This solved the problem but I was then back into non auto-stabilised flight which was a bit 'woolly' but controllable. After landing it was found that the technicians had wired up the pitch and yaw auto-stabs the wrong way around. It was all rather uncomfortable and it also showed that the wiring system was such that it could allow that sort of thing to happen.

After production testing I eventually moved onto the development side and a lot of my Buccaneer flying was then spent hovering close to the stall as we had to do low speed handling exercises for every different store and rack that came along so that an aerodynamic clearance could be given. To get meaningful figures for the Navy we started off at below 1,000 ft with full power and blow selected to simulate take-off conditions. The speed was gradually reduced by pulling the nose higher and higher until we got up to the height (usually around 8,000 ft) where the blow was reduced due to the fall off in atmospheric pressure. We would then descend and start the whole sequence again at a slightly lower speed. On a Buccaneer, of course, you made sure that you did not stall. If you did stall then the ejector seat was the only way out. It was also not recoverable from a spin; there was an occasion when one did come out of a spin from high level, but no one was really sure how it had been done.

Another thing that happened at the stall was that you tended to get pitch-up. Shortly before I joined Hawker Siddeley the Navy were having a problem with pitch-up after launch and a Buccaneer S.2 was lost [this was XN979 which crashed into the sea off Lizard Point shortly after launch on 9 June 1966. The crew ejected safely]. Lieutenant-Commander Dave Eagles was sent out to the Far East from Boscombe Down to show the Navy how to do the take off properly. An S.2 (XV153) was loaded to the same weight and launched from HMS *Victorious* at the same speed as the other aeroplane, but exactly the same thing happened and Dave and his observer had to eject. There was then an urgent development programme as it was realised that it was the aeroplane and not the pilots that was causing the problem. It turned out that the drop tanks had had a fairing put up to the leading edge of the wing and this was giving forward lift as it was moving the Centre of Pressure slightly forwards. We did a lot of testing up to what we called wing lowering (rather than wing drop) and this occurred normally at around 27 ADD. These were units rather than degrees and the ADD, which was an extremely useful device, told you when you were approaching the stall regardless of speed and weight. It had an audio facility for circuit work when the cockpit workload was high and although you always referred to the ASI as a cross reference, you could actually land without looking at the ASI at all.

The normal safe boundary in pitch was 24 ADD, anything above this figure was starting to get a bit dubious. It varied a little with different aeroplanes and I was once asked to fly a Buccaneer at Aldergrove as the Navy test pilot there would not clear it after servicing due to wing lowering. Derek Whitehead asked me if I would go over and test it and afterwards I had to write a very diplomatic report as the test pilot was quite right, it did have wing lowering, or wing drop as he called it. As an RAF aeroplane, however, this was really irrelevant as the Air Force did not go to the incidences that the Navy had to do when flying from carriers. I considered the aeroplane to be safe to fly on this basis, which seemed to satisfy everyone involved.

During the test flying that was done to clear underwing stores we also had to fly up to maximum 'g' and this involved doing wind-up turns. This was done by pulling into a turn and then dropping the nose to keep the speed up while maintaining the 'g'. One of these trips was done on a weekend and my observer (John Caulfield) was still a bit hung over from the night before. When we were in the high 'g' turn I looked in the rear view mirror and all I could see was the top of John's helmet. He was unconscious and my initial reaction was 'God, I've killed him!' I flew straight and level and kept shouting to him and eventually his head came up and he came round but he was not quite sure where he was. That was typical of blacking out with 'g' which went way beyond eye blacking out to the completely unconscious state.

In July 1972 I did the high weight take-off trials at Elvington which involved the heaviest ever flight in a Buccaneer at 61,300 lb (to put this into perspective, this is 90 per cent of the weight of a fully loaded Lancaster bomber). The take-off was fully blown at 30/20/20 configuration and as soon as the aeroplane was airborne you would retract the undercarriage, flap and aileron droop. Five seconds or so after the undercarriage had come up you would then cut one engine back to idle to prove single-engine safety. It was then a case of just sitting there with the airspeed not moving and waiting for the blow to cut off. When this happened the ADD increased as you were suddenly much closer to the stall, but with more thrust. I used to brief the observer before we did this particular test flight that if the ADD exceeded 24 units and was still going up, I would eject. That was the quickest way to tell him to eject and avoided him having to ask me as to whether or not I meant it. I used to say 'On the bottom of my boots is written the word "Goodbye" which you will see going over your head!'

Another aspect of testing was known as 'bonking'. On the Buccaneer we had special wing tips fitted which had slots for explosive cartridges, or bonkers, which were similar in size to those used in a twelve-bore gun. The idea was to put a jerk input into the aeroplane at a required airspeed and Mach number to check for freedom from the onset of flutter. This was done for every new store that came along and every weight change and involved climbing to a certain height, say 20,000 ft, and then diving to get the allotted Mach number and then holding that figure until it coincided with the airspeed you wanted. When that occurred the observer would then fire either symmetric (one each side) or asymmetric bonking. You would feel the bang in the aeroplane and the information from the strain gauges around the aeroplane would be analysed after landing to check that the traces were not about to expand and lead to flutter. I never had any problems during these particular trials, although we did have one occasion when all the bonkers went off together. During jettison trials we used wing tip mounted cameras to record the moment of release and I recall having to go down to 'C' Squadron at Boscombe Down as they had a Buccaneer that they thought was suffering from pitch-up. I did a low-speed handling check and found that the camera fairings that were fitted to this aeroplane had the effect of moving the Centre of Pressure forwards slightly which had affected the fore-and-aft stability. It did cross my mind that as Boscombe was full of test pilots, they might have been able to figure this out for themselves!

Although the Buccaneer could be affected by inertia coupling, I did not experience this particular phenomenon and if I had it would have led to an immediate ejection. To get around inertia coupling you were not allowed to do more than one roll at a time. If you did want to carry out more than one roll, for example during a display, you had to make sure that the controls were centralised and you flew straight and level for a short time before commencing the second roll, otherwise yaw coupling would result. This, I believe, was what happened to 'Sailor' Parker as he ran in over Holme-on-Spalding Moor and pulled up into a half loop with a roll off the top followed by another roll. He got yaw coupling and he and his observer (Gordon Copeman) were killed only yards from the Tower when the aeroplane went in [this accident occurred on 19 February 1963 and involved Buccaneer S.1 XN952].

Most Buccaneers were either lost in the circuit or to what was referred to as 'snatch pulling'. One incident I recall in particular was a Buccaneer which nearly collided with a Hunter over Wales. The pilot hauled back on the stick to avoid it but the aeroplane pitched up and stalled before crashing into a reservoir [this was XW525 of 208 Squadron which went down on 4 April 1977, the crew ejected safely]. At one time we experimented with various dampers to stop this happening and we spent quite a lot of time on it. We did practice snatch pulls to get the ADD a little higher each time to compare the results of different dampers, but nothing ever came of it as it was deemed to be too expensive. Another Buccaneer was lost shortly after we did these trials and I wrote to the Director of Flight Safety to say that I had never interfered in any accident before a Board of Inquiry result had come out, but in this case I felt sure I knew what had happened. I also said it would be far better if money was spent on fitting a proper stall warning device to the Buccaneer instead of messing about with dampers. I got a very nice letter back which was most sympathetic but it explained all the costs and the money that was available and I knew that the Buccaneer would get nothing.

I have always said that test flying is hours of boredom punctuated by seconds of sheer terror. The boring parts of the job are epitomised by fuel consumption checks where you have to sit for five minutes or so holding a speed to +/- 2 knots so that the technicians can get the accurate fuel consumption figures which end up in the Pilot's manual. As far as I am concerned the most dangerous parts of testing are low-speed handling trials, tests to determine maximum take-off and landing performance and the jettisoning of stores of any sort as they can always come back and strike the aeroplane. To discover landing performance you had to put the aeroplane on the runway and then apply brakes at the maximum permissible airspeed to get the shortest stopping distance which was asking for trouble from burst tyres, exploding wheels etc.

One of my worst moments in the air occurred on the range at West

Freugh near Stranraer during a jettison trial on 11 July 1979. This involved jettisoning a munitions dispenser during the trials to clear JP233 which was to be used by the Tornado GR.1. Our development Buccaneer (XK527) was the trials aeroplane but the firemen at West Freugh were on strike and the airfield was closed. Before I took off I rang Group Captain Chuck Charles at Farnborough to say that I had to do the trial as there was a lot of pressure to get it done and to enquire whether or not I could use the range there. He said that this would be possible except that I would not be able to land at West Freugh unless I had an emergency. I reminded him that I was flying a Buccaneer so fuel would not be a problem and I could easily make it back to Holme-on-Spalding Moor.

On arrival we did a dummy run over the range and then we flew in to do the live drop which was at 350 knots and 500 ft. As the store was jettisoned there was a bang as the explosive release worked but that was followed by a much bigger bang and the aeroplane shook violently. My observer said 'What's that', to which I replied 'It's hit us, but stay where you are we're still flying.' I looked at the instruments and they reverted to 99,000 ft and 0 knots so I looked out and the pitot head had gone from the left-hand wing and the tip was bent. I called West Freugh and said 'I now have an emergency.' We then climbed to 5,000 ft to test undercarriage, flap and droop, and tightened our straps in case we had to eject, but in the end we landed safely. If it had not been a Buccaneer with a stainless steel leading edge we would have been dead, as it would have taken the wing off. There would have been no chance of ejecting successfully from 500 ft as it would have rolled and we would have gone straight in.

After landing I rang Chuck Charles from the Tower to tell him what had happened and all he asked was that I go round to the Fire Section and thank the firemen for turning out. I went over to see the man in charge and he said 'Och, that's all right sir, only too glad to help.' Shortly afterwards the Dove arrived having picked up Ed Solman, the Head of Flight Test and another team who had come to look at the damage. They went straight into the hangar where we had put the Buccaneer. Ed walked in with a Polaroid camera and started taking pictures when a big chap dashed up, grabbed the camera and pulled the film out, saying 'You've got no permission to come filming in here.' It turned out that the official photographer at West Freugh was the union leader so I said to Ed 'Look you've tried to kill me again, I've solved the problem, appeased the firemen and you come along and spoil the whole thing.'

We did learn an important lesson from this particular incident and I changed the order book to say that in future the Chief Test Pilot would be shown and brought into the discussion about wind tunnel results. When I had the chance to look at these back at Brough I found that there had been a high probability of the store coming back and hitting the aeroplane. Probably as a result of pressure to get the trial done quickly I had been completely unaware of this.

Almost exactly a year before this incident I had been witness to a fatal accident in a Buccaneer. I was at West Freugh doing trials on the Pave Spike laser designator and I was cleared off the range one day as another aeroplane was coming on. I needed to burn off fuel to get down to landing weight so I was cleared to do this in the circuit. We saw the other aeroplane coming up the range in the distance and he appeared to have plenty of power on as there was black smoke behind it. Mike Nicholl, my observer, kept an eye on it and mentioned that it was another Buccaneer. I then landed and was taxiing back up the runway when Mike said that the other aeroplane was going in. I looked up and saw it in a steep nose-down attitude and it seemed to take ages before it disappeared into the ground. The navigator tried to eject at the last moment; I saw his seat come out but by that time it was way too late. It was all a bit shattering as it had come down right on the edge of the airfield. It turned out that the pilot was Alan Love who was doing testing work at Warton. I had known him as a Flying Officer when he was on Hunters at Duxford. He had been cleared to carry on with his run but he was to remain clear of the circuit. I reckoned that he was trying his best to get on the green 'soft' target and obviously pulled round tight to keep out of the circuit and stalled it. One of the ironies of this whole episode was that the navigator, a former Lieutenant-Commander in the Royal Navy, had asked me for a job the month before as he was not happy at Warton [the Buccaneer involved in this accident was XT285 which had been modified to take part in the Tornado development programme].

During my time at HSA/BAe I took part in a number of weapons trials including Martel and Sidewinder and I was involved in Sea Eagle from the start. One of the trials on Sea Eagle was tethered engine firing which was carried out on XK527. This involved firing the engine of the missile while it was still attached to the wing of the Buccaneer to check that it worked correctly. I did the first ever Sea Eagle firing over Cardigan Bay on 24 April 1981 in XW529. I had a chase aeroplane that day and the weather on take off from Holme-on-Spalding Moor was foul. We joined up above cloud and the idea was that I would fire the missile over the sea and the other aeroplane would formate on it. Unfortunately the weather was not much better over Wales and he lost it in the murk.

My last ever flight in a Buccaneer was in XW529 on 20 September 1982 with Jim Nottingham in the back. This was a flight from Holme-on-Spalding Moor to Hatfield which was being used for development of the Sea Eagle missile and had had runway arrestor gear put in, at great expense, to allow Buccaneer operations to be carried out from there. It was a sad occasion when I stepped out of a Buccaneer for the final time having accumulated a total of 1,064 hours on type. It was a superb aeroplane that was ideally suited to the role for which it was designed and it is a privilege to have flown it.

Don Headley retired from test flying in 1982 remaining with British Aerospace until 1988. However, he was to return to the world of flight testing when he took over the role of Chief Test Pilot at Slingsby Aviation Ltd at Kirkbymoorside. Here he was able to bring his considerable expertise to the development of the single-engined T.67M Firefly *ab initio* trainer. At the time of writing he has just brought his career in aviation to an end after fifty-five years in the air.

AAA	Anti-aircraft Artillery
A&AEE	Aeroplane and Armament Experimental Establishment
AAM	Air-to-air Missile
AAR	Air-to-air Refuelling
ADD	Airstream Direction Detector
ADDL	Aerodrome Dummy Deck Landing
ADSL	Automatic Depressed Sightline
AEW	Airborne Early Warning
AGL	Above Ground Level
AR	Anti Radar (or anti-radiation)
ASL	Above Sea Level
ASM	Air-to-surface Missile
AUW	All-up weight
BLC	Boundary Layer Control
CAP	Combat Air Patrol
CFS	Central Flying School
CG	Centre of Gravity
CMRP	Continuous Mosaic Radar Prediction
CRT	Cathode Ray Tube
CSI	Combined Speed Indicator
CTTO	Central Tactics and Trials Organisation
DR	Dead Reckoning
ECM	Electronic Countermeasures
FCR	Fire Control Radar
FDO	Flight Deck Officer
FI	Fatigue Index
Flyco	Flying control position overlooking the flight deck on an aircraft carrier
GCI	Ground Controlled Interception
GPI	Ground Position Indicator
HP	High Pressure
IAS	Indicated Airspeed

IFF	Identification Friend or Foe
IFIS	Integrated Flight Instrumentation System
IMC	Instrument Meteorological Conditions
IMN	Indicated Mach Number
IR	Infra-red
ISA	International Standard Atmosphere
JPT	Jet Pipe Temperature
LABS	Low Altitude Bombing System
LGB	Laser Guided Bomb
LODT	Locked On Dive Toss
MDSL	Manual Depressed Sightline
MRE	Monopulse Resolution Enhancement
MRG	Master Reference Gyro
MSDS	Marconi Space and Defence Systems
NAS	Naval Air Station
NATO	North Atlantic Treaty Organisation
NM	Nautical Miles
OCU	Operational Conversion Unit
PCU	Power Control Unit
PEC	Personal Equipment Connector
PSI	Pounds per Square Inch
PSP	Personal Survival Pack
QFI	Qualified Flying Instructor
QRB	Quick Release Button
PIO	Pilot Induced Oscillation
PLM	Post Launch Manoeuvre
PPI	Plan Position Indicator
PWR	Passive Warning Radar
RP	Rocket Projectile
RPM	Revolutions Per Minute
RRADSL	Radar Range Automatic Depressed Sightline
RT	Radio Transmitter

SAG	Surface Action Group
SAM	Surface-to-air Missile
SARH	Semi-active Radar Homing
SFI	Special Flying Instruction
SSM	Surface-to-surface missile
SWP	Standard Warning Panel
TACAN	Tactical Air Navigation
TAS	True Airspeed
TBO	Time Between Overhauls
TGT	Turbine Gas Temperature
TMC	Target Marker Computer
TMN	True Mach Number
VMC	Visual Meteorological Conditions

Buccaneer S.2
Selected Emergency Procedures

The following is taken from the Flight Reference Cards for the Buccaneer S.2 Issue 3 dated April 1967

ENGINE FAILURES

One Engine Failure During Take-off
Take-off abandoned
Close HP cocks
Lower arrester hook
Extend airbrakes
Apply wheel brakes
Aim for centre of wires
Immediately prior to engagement release wheel brakes and pull stick back

Take-off continued
Moderate application of rudder is required to keep straight
Fly off at the unstick speed +15 knots blown or unstick speed +10 knots unblown
Raise the undercarriage and the flap/droop configuration
Allow the speed to increase and climb away

One Engine Failure After Take-off
The aircraft will climb away after unstick if unblown and will climb away blown if the safety speed below has been reached

42,000 lb – 165 knots
47,000 lb – 172 knots
51,000 lb – 180 knots

Raise the undercarriage and flap/droop configuration. Allow the speed to increase and climb away. Moderate application of rudder is required to oppose the yaw. Control movements, to oppose yaw and a tendency to roll, should be made gently and kept to a minimum

Engine Failure in Flight
Flame-out
Attempt relight immediately
If unsuccessful, close HP cock and relight as required

Double flame-out
Attempt immediate relight on both engines
Maintain minimum airspeed of 250 knots or 13 per cent windmilling RPM for flying controls
If no relight, close HP cocks and isolate generator
Descend before attempting a further relight

Fuel management
Open inter-tank transfer valves
Close FNA valves on live engine side. Reopen the FNA valves before contents of either master tank on the dead side shows 75 lb and immediately close inter-tank transfer valves
Any fuel remaining on the dead engine will be unusable

Engine Overheating
Indication
The associated engine overheat warning light illuminates

Actions
Reduce power. If warning light goes out, the engine may be used judiciously at reduced power
If warning light remains on then:
Close HP cock
Close engine master fuel cock

Considerations
The fire extinguishers must not be used
The engine must not be restarted

One Engine Failure on Approach
At 34,500 lb AUW safety height is 200 ft at datum speed

Above safety height
If it is necessary to overshoot ease stick forward, apply full power on live engine, retract airbrakes
Increase speed to datum speed + 5 knots
Raise the undercarriage
Select configuration to 30/20/20

Rotate to level flight as new datum speed is reached
Select configuration to 15/10/10, climb away

Below safety height
To land, ease stick forward, apply full power on live engine, retract airbrakes, maintain at least datum speed
Do not raise the undercarriage

Mechanical failure in flight
Immediate actions
Close HP and master cocks of associated engine

Considerations
Depending on extent of failure, fire may follow. In most cases it is better to reduce speed and operate fire extinguisher

SINGLE ENGINE FLIGHT
WARNING – Flight in icing conditions should be avoided due to lack of anti-icing protection for the dead engine
To stop engine:
HP cock – OFF
Generator switch – OFF

Services lost (if windmilling RPM below 13 per cent)

Port engine stopped
No autostab on rudder (switch on yaw damper)
No autostab on tailplane or port aileron
No autopilot on port aileron and tailplane

Starboard engine stopped
No autostab or autopilot on starboard aileron
No Q-feel or yaw damper
No autopilot heading hold
Remainder continue to operate

Fuel management
Deliberate single-engine flight
Shut down and restart each engine in turn
Leave equal fuel in both sides for a two-engine recovery

Relighting in flight
Optimum speed – 250 to 300 knots
Height band – Sea Level to 25,000 ft

Relight procedure
Engine master cock on
Press the relight button and open the HP cock
When RPM and TGT start to rise, release the relight button
Switch on the generator
When the engine runs satisfactorily open the throttle slowly to the required RPM
Check –
TGT – not above 600 degrees C
Oil pressure MI – cross-hatched (min) by 65 per cent RPM
Fire warning light – Out

If there is no light-up within 20 seconds, release relight button and close HP cock. Allow engine to drain for 1 minute before making a second attempt at a lower altitude. If engine relights but RPM stagnates below flight idling, increase speed as necessary to assist RPM to build up. If, after 1 minute, the engine appears unlikely to pull away, close HP cock, allow engine to drain before making another attempt

Circuit and landing (max AUW 36,000 lb)
Normal circuit at 1,000 ft, blow on. Restrict flap configuration to 30/20/20
Lower undercarriage. Set approximately 92 per cent RPM (89 per cent minimum for blow)
Make a long straight approach
Adjust speed by use of airbrakes, turn crosswind at datum speed +10 knots
Maintain datum speed throughout approach
Carry out a normal landing. Do not reduce power until after touchdown

Single engine overshoot
Decision height – 200 ft at datum speed
Apply full power on live engine, close airbrakes and raise undercarriage
As airbrakes close, anticipate increased yaw towards dead engine
Climb initially at datum speed
When safely climbing, increase speed by 10 knots for improved rate of climb
NOTE 1 – At a weight of 42,000 lb or less the aircraft will overshoot from the runway in the unblown configuration
NOTE 2 – At 36,000 lb and below in the blown configuration, the aircraft will overshoot satisfactorily at datum speed from the runway

ENGINE FIRE IN FLIGHT
Indications

The fire warning lights on the SWP and in the appropriate fire extinguisher button will come on.

Immediate actions

Close HP and master cocks of affected engine and, if possible, reduce speed before operating fire extinguisher button

Subsequent actions if warnings remain on:

Check for confirmatory evidence of fire (instruments, cockpit conditions, behaviour of flying controls, outside evidence etc) and if fire is confirmed, abandon aircraft

If fire is not confirmed, land as soon as possible, being prepared to abandon at any time

Subsequent actions if warnings cancel:

Set 100 per cent oxygen

If necessary, due to fumes etc, switch off pressurisation and open ram air valve

Considerations

Do not relight engine

WARNING – if an engine and a fuel bay fire are indicated and the warnings do not cancel within 5 seconds, abandon the aircraft

FIRE IN BOMB BAY AND FUEL TANK AREA
Indications

FIRE B or FIRE F warnings on SWP

Actions

Extinguishers operate automatically and SWP warning cancels when temperature has reduced. If SWP warning does not cancel in 4 to 5 seconds, abandon the aircraft

WARNING – if an engine and a fuel bay fire are indicated and the warnings do not cancel within 5 seconds, abandon the aircraft

CANOPY JETTISONING

Observer lowers seat fully, hands adjacent to firing handle

Pilot operates canopy jettison handle

After canopy has gone, noise level high, aircrew vision impaired by dirt sucked up from cockpit, observer subject to buffet and may have to use seat pan firing handle (pre Mod 871). Post Mod 871 observer can use either handle up to 500 knots, above that speed the seat will have to be lowered to the mid or lower positions before the face-blind handle can be reached. Intercom is not possible above 250 knots

ABANDONING THE AIRCRAFT

Optimum speed – 250 knots

Ground level ejection
From straight and level flight
Minimum airspeed – 90 knots
Maximum airspeed – 350 knots at 0 ft, 600 knots at 100 ft. If possible convert speed to height

Ejection at altitude
Reduce speed to 230 knots
Note altitude
Initiate distress procedure
Jettison canopy
Position body correctly before initiating ejection
If seat fails to eject:
Release the safety catch and pull the manual separation handle upwards to its full extent (Mks I and II seats only)
Grasping parachute lift webs above and behind shoulders, lean forward pulling pack forward onto shoulders
Transfer both sets of lift webs to one hand
Action as at (1) (Mk III seat only)
Pilot inverts aircraft and applies negative-G
When clear of aircraft pull rip-cord D-ring. If (5) not possible
Using free hand, pull body up and clear dinghy pack from seat pan, at the same time easing forward so that pack resets on edge of seat pan
Turn and face either side of aircraft, avoiding slipstream and preventing parachute snagging objects in cockpit, by holding close to shoulders
Stand up holding PEC clear and dive over the side
When clear of aircraft, pull rip-cord D-ring

NOTE – no oxygen is available after a manual bale-out

Failure of automatic separation
Release safety catch and operate manual separation lever
Push clear of seat
Pull rip-cord handle
Controlled ejection
Aircraft – Clean
Height – 9,000 ft
Power – Idling RPM
Speed – 230 knots
Trim tailplane for level flight
Apply 1 division of aileron trim

Position aircraft with selected crash area 30 degrees on bow, range 2 miles
Jettison canopy
Order observer 'Eject, Eject'
Release controls and eject

DITCHING
WARNING – It is always advisable to eject rather than to ditch. With double-engine failure it is essential to abandon

If ejection is not possible
Jettison external stores and canopy whilst in the air, then
Oxygen – 100 per cent selected. Deflect emergency toggle. Depress mask toggle
Approach in the landing flap/droop configuration with undercarriage and airbrake retracted at 24 units on the ADD indicator. Land into wind or along swell if swell is steep.
WARNING – If time does not permit the above actions, jettison canopy whilst on the surface. If the aircraft sinks with the canopy in position, abandoning, using either underwater escape system or normal ejection, will be hazardous

Canopy off
Action when aircraft sinks
Brace head and shoulders, operate underwater escape firing handle
After escaping remove oxygen mask, release QRB, free harness, disconnect PSP and inflate life-raft
Action if underwater escape system fails
Release QRB and free harness, release PSP
Climb out, inflate LSW, remove oxygen mask and inflate life-raft

Canopy on
Action whether aircraft floats or sinks
Brace head and shoulders, operate underwater escape firing handle. After escaping remove oxygen mask, release QRB, free harness, disconnect PSP and inflate life-raft
Action if underwater escape system fails
Wait until canopy is submerged
Brace head and shoulders, operate normal ejection seat firing handle
Remove oxygen mask, inflate LSW, release QRB, free harness, disconnect PSP and inflate life-raft.

INDEX